Couples in Counselling

Couples in Counselling

A Consumer's Guide to
Marriage Counselling

TONY GOUGH

Darton, Longman and Todd
London

First published in 1989 by
Darton, Longman and Todd Ltd
89 Lillie Road, London SW6 1UD

British Library Cataloguing in Publication Data

Gough, Tony
Couples in counselling: a consumer's guide
to marriage counselling.
1. Marriage counselling
I. Title
362.8'286

ISBN 0-232-51826-2

The quotations introducing the four parts of this book are taken from Sheldon Kopp's *Who Am I – Really?* (Jeremy P. Tarcher Inc. 1987).

Phototypeset by Input Typesetting Ltd, London
Printed and bound in Great Britain by
Anchor Press Ltd, Tiptee, Essex

For my daughters and their partners,
Sue and Paul,
Jill and Kevin,
Deb and Neil,
Liz and Bruno
and for little Katie Jennifer who, at 5½,
has plenty of time to make up her mind about
her future soul-friend,
With my love, as ever

Contents

Acknowledgements

In writing this book, I owe an enormous debt of gratitude to my many teachers over the years, most especially the countless couples whom I have counselled during the past thirty years or so. They have taught me so much; through their pain and struggle they can at least have the satisfaction of knowing that they have helped to help others.

I am most grateful to Moira Fryer of RELATE for reading the original manuscript and for making various suggestions regarding the shape and content of the material. Her comments were incisive and valuable. I also thank the other readers who helped me find a better path through the enormous amount of material I started out with, and who encouraged me to leave some of the luggage behind! I also thank Jean Judge and her staff at the Catholic Marriage Advisory Council who supplied information. The staff at the *Leicester Mercury* library were tremendously helpful in digging out the various news items referred to.

I also gladly acknowledge the regular support, love and caring confrontation I receive through my own supervision group – Ted Kettell, Hazel Marshall and Lois Tait – who encourage me in my work. The wisdom and constant support of my consultant supervisor, Dr David Toms, is a resource upon which it would be impossible to place a value. Thank you all.

Finally, I must thank my wife, Jan, for her continual help and practical suggestions made in presenting this material. She has an unerring sense of whether, after counselling, I need coffee, sherry or a stiff gin and tonic! She is also a perceptive counsellor and her partnership sustains me daily.

Western Park
Leicester
November 1988

Tony Gough

Introduction

As a professional counsellor, I cannot approach this subject of couples in counselling with complete detachment and an unbiased mind. So I declare my interest at the outset. Having said that, I also firmly believe that the skills which counsellors use are none other than *ordinary* human gifts of caring, listening and understanding. These are not the property of any professional clique. They belong to the world of human relationships and form the major ingredients of any satisfactory way of relating to one another.

That things can go drastically wrong with our most intimate relationships is obvious to those of us who have taken the risk of committing ourselves to another person. In my book, *Couples Arguing* (what one radio interviewer called 'The Good Row Guide'), I set out some practical guidelines for improving the ways we communicate with one another, especially as they concern our innermost thoughts and feelings. All the major surveys concerning intimate relationships stress the need for better communication between couples. *Couples Arguing* apparently broke new ground in Great Britain in the important areas of self-expression and creative conflict.

But not all the conflict between couples can be described as 'creative'. Much of it is utterly destructive and, frankly, there are times when we want it to be so. We want to lash out and hurt the other person, and some of us have found effective ways of hurting people we love. In the process we find ourselves in a battered relationship, and wonder what to do about healing it. It might be that you have picked this book up in a state of desperation concerning your most important relationship. You want to know if counselling might possibly help you and your partner find a way forward out of a situation which seems beyond the reach of self-help alone.

There are other things you may also want to know:
How does counselling work and who are the people who need counselling?
What kind of problems do people most frequently bring into counselling?
What actually goes on at a counselling session, and where can I find the most appropriate help for me?

These are some of the basic questions which people in pain often ask, and which I have tried to answer in this book. My chief aim has been to make counselling more accessible to the general public and to explain how it works out in practice.

I believe this to be an urgent and necessary task. Through my own counselling practice, I am continually being reminded of the amount of pain and misery borne by people suffering from ordinary human unhappiness. Much of this unhappiness occurs through painful relationships. The effect is, of course, nationwide. It is certainly far beyond the bare divorce statistics. Although these figures showed a drop in 1987 (165,000 compared with 175,000 in 1985), divorces involve over 300,000 people annually; and when you add to that the number of children of those marriages and other members of their families, it is not alarmist to assume that over a million individuals get caught up in this painful leave-taking process every year. This figure does not include those who choose to separate without subsequent divorce.

If any other social malaise were to involve more than a million people a year, there would be a public outcry that 'something should be done about it!' As a leading article in *The Times* (6 Feb. 1988) said,

> If it were a virus that was attacking marriages, epidemiological studies and laboratory research would proceed apace, and public health and public education measures could expect adequate government support. That is exactly what has happened in the case of AIDS, and rightly so. The incidence of marriage breakdown is in its own way a catastrophe: it demands some priority too.

Yet, apparently, ordinary human unhappiness does not fall within any such priority. It is merely regarded as inevitable and incurable.

Some of the more desperately unhappy people will show physical symptoms (the psychosomatic illnesses) and these may claim the attention of those working in the National Health Service. General practitioners, hospital consultants and specialists in conditions of stress will say there are no *organic* reasons why these symptoms are cropping up so regularly. Feelings of anxiety, tension, depression, stress and the complicated world of the phobic patient, are no stranger to the doctors' surgeries. One report on breast cancer (which claims the lives of 14,000 British women every year) suggests that it is being statistically linked to stressful events in their lives and an inability to cope with them. According to Professor Cary Cooper, the head of organizational psychology at the University of Manchester, the medical profession has been extremely slow at recognizing the effect of psycho-social factors on health and well-being. He says, 'If you cry, do not cry alone. Do it when other people are around so that someone will see that you are upset and will listen to you. If that is difficult, seek other help; *counselling will do you much more good than Valium*' (my italics).

It may be that the work undertaken by the NHS which is stress-originated is costed somewhere; it must run into billions of pounds each year. The bill for tranquillizers alone is astronomical. In a world increasingly governed by economic considerations, the cost of ordinary human unhappiness deserves more attention. But is it receiving that extra attention?

Some important changes are now beginning to occur that will, in time, significantly alter this situation. Within the NHS itself, trained counsellors and psychotherapists are joining the ranks of those involved in primary mental health care. Their long waiting-lists indicate how much such a service is in demand, and more urgent funding is a necessity. Unfortunately, spending on mental health care in our community has always been the 'Cinderella' of the NHS, but any new resources, however limited, are welcome. More counsellors are also being employed at local health care centres, and in the near future it is hoped that patients will have access to a trained counsellor at their own local doctor's surgery.

This change within the medical profession itself has been brought about by improvements in the way in which our general practitioners are trained. The long-term results of this new approach by doctors to people in pain will radically alter the way medicine is being practised in our country. Doctors who have espoused the 'holistic' medical stance (which looks at people first, rather than just their presenting symptoms) are becoming widespread in our local surgeries, and their impact is being felt. One of the sub-groups within the British Association for Counselling deals specifically with counselling in medical settings, and this is a valuable resource both to the doctors who employ counsellors and the counsellors themselves.

Then there are the specific counselling agencies which are becoming widely known. I contacted two of the better known agencies who specialize in marriage counselling for the purpose of background research for this book. Their statistics make interesting reading.

RELATE (the National Marriage Guidance Council), for instance, which is the largest matrimonial counselling agency in Great Britain, interviewed 377,000 people in 1987. The Catholic Marriage Advisory Council held over 20,000 interviews in 1985/6. Some people were seen individually, some as couples, and the demand on the services of these agencies is rising all over the country. How has this current demand for counselling come about? To be sure, it is not by high-pressured salesmanship. People are beginning to break through the traditional British reserve towards counselling, and it is interesting to find out how this has happened.

Until fairly recently, certainly into the early 1980s, counselling has been seen as a rather dubious *American* activity, which was enough to damn the whole enterprise in the eyes of many British people! However, three national tragedies, each attracting wide publicity and public sympathy, seem to have effected a radical shift in these old-fashioned attitudes to counselling.

In May 1985 there was a tragic fire at the Bradford City football ground, in which fifty-five people lost their lives and many more were injured. Such was the widespread shock throughout Bradford that a city-wide counselling programme was set up in order to help people affected either personally or emotionally by this disaster. It was the first time that a counselling programme had been set up to deal with the emotional reactions of a whole community. This attracted much attention and proved its usefulness to many people who availed themselves of this special kind of help. Perhaps not surprisingly, a similar programme, headed by some of the Bradford counselling team, was used on the occasion of another national tragedy, that of the sinking of the Herald of Free Enterprise ferry off Zeebrugge in March 1987. Headquarters were set up in Dover to deal with the many relatives and others affected by this appalling accident which claimed the lives of 193 people. At least there was someone to listen to those people who needed help in coming to terms with what had happened, whether or not they had lost relatives on the boat. The third event concerned the massacre of sixteen people in the small Berkshire town of Hungerford in August 1987, when a deranged man went on an apparently senseless rampage and in the space of a few hours wreaked havoc on a quiet rural town. Once again, counselling facilities were set up and those who had felt devastated by the experience of shock and horror could talk to trained helpers about their feelings. Social workers and police psychologists were called in to help in Hungerford, although in fact the shock-waves of this particular disaster affected the whole of the nation, since such insane massacres were virtually unknown in this country.

In my opinion, Bradford, Zeebrugge, and Hungerford have, once and for all, changed British attitudes towards the acceptability and credibility of the counselling process. No longer need counselling be thought of as provision for a bunch of weirdos or social inadequates. The value to those who sought the help of these counselling agencies at their time of stress has been incalculable. Permission to feel and express deep emotions which these tragedies evoked in people proved to be a help on the road to healing. The concept of the 'caring community' was set forward by this imaginative and well-organized counselling service.

Such a transformation of national opinion did not, of course, appear out of the blue. For the past twenty years (at least) there has been a steady growth in the 'counselling industry' (as a Radio 4 broadcast called it). Through this growth many people, who formerly would not have considered that counselling was either appropriate or available, have been helped during their personal life crises. Hitherto, private psychotherapy or counselling was generally considered to be for the seriously disturbed or mentally ill, and it was mainly for those with means to pay for it. That image must now give way in the light of the disasters mentioned above.*

So, if you or your partner are considering marriage counselling, you will no longer find yourselves taking part in some questionable activity. The chances are that someone you know, who themselves have been involved in counselling, has recommended this course of action to you. However, your fears and apprehensions about counselling are entirely appropriate, and I hope that what I have written in this 'Consumer's Guide to Marriage Counselling' will help to allay enough of those fears for you to find out for yourself.

As will be apparent throughout this book, I have written it in the course of a busy counselling practice. This has provided much of the day-to-day clinical material contained in the book. I am deeply conscious of the need for anonymity, and I have therefore taken pains to ensure the total confidentiality of my clients, as consistent with the code of ethics within which I work. At least you will be encouraged to find my feet planted firmly in the world of real people in pain, and may judge for yourself my caring responses to them.

Should this book enable you to take the risk of getting into the counselling process, and thereby learn more constructive ways of relating to your partner and finding new ways of self-fulfilment and happiness within your marriage, my efforts will have been more than rewarded.

* Since writing this, we need to add to those mentioned the Piper Alpha North Sea explosion, the rail crash at Clapham Junction (Nov. 1988), the Lockerbie air crash (Dec. 1988) and the M1 air crash (Jan. 1989). All of these disasters were responded to with counselling facilities.

PART 1: HOW DOES COUNSELLING WORK?

Revealing myself to others always involves taking a chance. But hiding out can be just as risky.

1 Towards a definition

Counselling has recently experienced liberation from its former (and erroneous) association with serious mental illness or chronic inadequacy. However, in the process of setting this word free from such associations, it has acquired a number of different meanings. 'Financial counselling', 'abortion counselling', 'sterilization counselling', and other specialized forms of counselling all contain a strong emphasis on 'being told what to do'. 'Marriage counselling' or 'problem counselling', however, has a somewhat different emphasis.

There are a number of emphases in the counselling basket. *Therapy* comes from a Greek word for 'healing', and this can sometimes be used in place of the word 'counselling'. This is certainly true in the United States where 'going into therapy' is as normal as going to the dentist. (You also see this word at the end of other words, such as physio*therapy* and psycho*therapy*, with connotations of bodily and mental healing.)

Befriending is another 'in-word' which refers mainly to a non-professional approach to helping people. This is not to imply a patronizing attitude towards befriending, as if to say, 'That's OK for the amateur!' There is a genuine place for such non-professional help, and in some communities it would simply be called good neighbourliness. Such help does in fact go on in homes and relationships without any consciousness that the helper is acting within a role. Whenever one person is available to listen to and understand another person in difficulty or pain, then befriending is in operation.

Telephone counselling has been the special genius of the voluntary organization known as the Samaritans, founded by the Rev. Chad Varah. This form of counselling focuses upon crisis intervention and is probably the best known of all the counselling agencies. The work of the Samaritans has been of great value to many thousands of people, not least the suicidal, and they are very often the first people called upon in a family or personal crisis. Part of the attraction of such help is that it is (or can be) entirely anonymous, which is not the same as saying it is impersonal. Quite the reverse. In fact, there are now many other 'hot-line' agencies available, specializing in all kinds of help. Among the better known are the various AIDS telephone numbers for enquirers, and the Child-Line facility for children suffering from physical or sexual abuse. If evidence were needed of the amount of sheer desperation in our society, these two agencies alone would provide it. To feel cared for in a time of crisis, and to be listened to without criticism or blame, is a healing experience.

No single definition of counselling is going to please everyone, especially my professional colleagues with their particular preferences and training; nevertheless, I will make an attempt to outline my own personal understanding. Since many of you might be strangers to the realm of counselling, it might be useful for me to begin by saying what counselling is *not*.

Counselling is not giving advice. This is, perhaps, the most frequent misunderstanding of the counselling process. Many couples find themselves at their wits' end in their marriage, and the urge to seek someone to tell them what to do is understandable enough. But think for a moment of the implications of giving another person advice either about their marriage or any other problem they might have.

1. *There is the strong implication that the counsellor has all the answers.* People often project on to the counselling process the medical model which works on the basis of 'you have symptom; I have prescription'. The truth is that counsellors do not possess all the answers to life's problems – ask them if you don't believe me. By the way, if you happen to meet one who says they DO have all the answers, *avoid them like the plague.* As Sheldon Kopp notes:

The Zen Master warns: 'If you meet the Buddha on the road,

> kill him!' This admonition points up that no meaning that comes from outside of ourselves is real. The Buddhahood of each of us has already been obtained. We need only recognize it . . . The only meaning in our lives is what we each bring to them. Killing the Buddha on the road means destroying the hope that anything outside ourselves can be our master.[1]

2. *There is the unspoken assumption that in some way the couple is unable to find satisfactory solutions to their own problems.* For those people who have had all the confidence knocked out of them through some painful life experience, it is natural (if mistaken) to assume that they are totally without resources. For anyone – counsellor, friend or neighbour – to dive in with instant solutions to problems which are scarcely defined or understood, is a highly dangerous thing to do. The assumption of the 'one-up, one-down' counselling relationship is then totally reinforced; the idea that power and resourcefulness somehow lie outside the person seeking help – in this case, within the counsellor or helper – is thereby taken for granted. It is, in my opinion, not helpful in the long run to reinforce a person's sense of inferiority or helplessness. Why start down a path which emphasizes a person's weakness, when healing lies in a totally different direction?

3. *Advice-giving tends towards adding to a couple's sense of dependency.* Some people have been taught by life's painful experiences to rely on others. Helpless themselves, they must find a dependent 'other' upon whom they can lean at times of stress, crisis and need. Sometimes this sense of dependency reaches chronic proportions. Defining themselves as 'victims' they search frantically for a 'rescuer'. Many clients come into counselling with this 'me-victim, you-rescuer' script. It is one of the first fantasies to be challenged within any on-going counselling relationship. If I, as counsellor, allow myself to be fooled into believing that you are a helpless victim, and that I am an all-powerful, all-knowing rescuer, we are both going to end up in Cloud-Cuckoo-Land. Worse, my rescue act will *ensure* that you will always remain a victim. In other words, counselling will in no way have strengthened you so that you will be able to cope more adequately with future problems; rescuing ensures that you will come back to be rescued every time you face

a crisis. It often comes as a shock to couples in counselling to discover that their counsellor does not have all the answers, if indeed he or she has any. In fact, like the patient who is not given a prescription by their GP, some couples believe themselves to have been deceived and cheated when they fail to get advice in counselling. Such people simply go elsewhere, taking with them their problematical shopping-basket for someone else to fill.

4. Another reason why the 'advice-giving' type of counselling is unhelpful, if not dangerous, is that *responsibility for the successful outcome of the counselling sessions relies solely upon what the counsellor does*. In other words, the only learning experience the couple has is in discovering how powerful/wonderful/marvellous/clever the counsellor is! This can hardly be a satisfactory aim in any kind of counselling. Should counselling fail to address itself to the innate sense of inadequacy in the couple seeking help then it would be better for them not to have that counselling at all. Counselling is about enabling other people to take responsibility for themselves, not about passively accepting whatever good ideas counsellors might have up their professional sleeves.

5. *Advice-giving lays itself open to attack and blame should the advice given go wrong*. Should the couple accept the advice of the counsellor, and their subsequent actions result in some disastrous failure, the counsellor will be held responsible. 'Fat lot of good your advice was!' will be the well-deserved response. Some people, of course, are very insistent that they get such advice – 'That's what we've come here for!' – and they need to understand that that is not what counselling is about. Such advice might well be at the heart of some forms of counselling (e.g. financial, legal, medical) but it is entirely out of place in any form of psychotherapeutic counselling worth its name.

I have dealt with what I consider counselling is *not*. Now I will turn to what I believe true counselling is about.

1. *Counselling is about enabling you to find satisfactory solutions to your own problems*. Note the word 'enabling'. It is at the heart of all

true counselling. To enable another person is *not* to do something *for* them. I am often asked by couples, 'Can you do anything for us?', to which my usual reply is, 'No, not a thing! I will do nothing *for* you, but I will try and do something *with* you.' Is this merely playing with words? I think not. There is all the difference in the world between my doing something for you and doing something with you. 'Doing for' is rescuing; 'doing with' is enabling you to help yourself. This idea was, for me, summed up in a brilliant Oxfam poster many years ago. It said,

GIVE A MAN A FISH AND YOU FEED HIM FOR A DAY;
TEACH A MAN TO FISH AND YOU FEED HIM FOR LIFE.

I have little sympathy with those types of counselling which are reluctant to show other people how to use a fishing rod for themselves. It might do wonders for the counsellor's ego, but it does nothing apart from reinforce dependency patterns of behaviour in those who seek their help. Enabling, on the other hand, challenges the inherent sense of helplessness in many couples who seek marriage counselling. The *fact* that my clients think that I have all the answers is significant in itself. It is one of their assumptions which must be dealt with at the beginning of the counselling process, but with a sympathetic understanding. Others, of course, are glad that I make no claims to infallibility and that my role is to assist them in finding their own solutions to their problems. This 'teaching them to fish' approach is rooted in another important aspect of counselling, namely –

2. *Respect*. It seems to me that to show respect to another human being, no matter in what state of temporary helplessness they might find themselves, is crucial to the advancement of human values in our society. This respect is twofold: first, for the couple; secondly, for the counsellor's own integrity. Respect ensures that couples are neither thought of, nor treated as, hopeless inadequates. It ensures the removal of any residue of patronizing attitudes which the counsellor might be tempted to adopt towards those they seek to help. Respect needs to be shown especially towards those who feel that they have lost all their sense of self-respect. Some individuals and couples feel they have forfeited

their sense of self-respect through their own actions (for example, husbands who have battered their wives or wives who have committed adultery). In such instances it is vital for the counsellor to treat their clients with respect for the pain they feel and the guilt they often harbour. Not to be thought of as stupid or insane or beyond help is of great therapeutic significance to those who come into counselling. It is equally important for the *counsellor's* sense of self-respect not to get hooked into regarding people as *cases*. It is not easy to evoke in others a sense of self-respect if it is manifestly lacking in the helper herself. If I diminish another person I am in fact diminishing myself. If I treat others as less than human I am treating myself as less than human, because, as John Donne reminds us, 'Any man's death diminishes me, because I am involved in Mankind'.[2] Conversely, in giving my clients an attitude of respect, I am also respecting my own integrity. It keeps me in my place.

3. *Counselling is about helping you to work towards a fuller understanding of your own personal problems.* It has less to do with supplying 'off the peg' solutions, and more to do with a much slower, yet essential, process of examining the problem of the couple concerned. One of the basic tasks of counselling is to invite the couple to explore more fully the problem by which they feel baffled. First, I might ask, 'Why is this a problem at all?' (a daft question you might think but one necessary to ask at the outset of the counselling relationship). Or I ask, 'Whose problem is it?' to determine the feelings of the main complainer. It is also important to ascertain the degree of understanding and sympathy (or lack of them!) by the other partner. Gradually a picture emerges of how deep and wide the underlying problems really are and of the couple's traditional ways of either avoiding them or dealing with them. What might start out as the 'presenting problem' actually goes much deeper than the couple realize.

4. *Counselling also involves an invitation to change.* This can be a most threatening process for many couples, however necessary they discover it to be. I sometimes compare my counselling room to one of those changing rooms you find in some large department stores. Taking three or four new items from the many displayed

in the shop, you go to the changing room to try them on. 'How do I feel in this one?', you ask yourself or your partner. 'Does this one feel right?', you wonder. 'How will this change my image?' Trying on several models you have an opportunity of enlarging your self-concept and self-expression by simply experimenting with various colours, textures and designs you have never tried before. All this is true of counselling. Couples in my 'changing room' can similarly try on different styles, not in terms of dress but of behaviour. Couples can experiment with a variety of new styles of relating and responding to one another. The *necessity* for change is not hard to find. Since the existing unhappiness is emerging as a direct result of their current ways of relating to one another, no improvement in that relationship is going to be seen until they decide upon some fundamental changes. What those changes are will undoubtedly be aired with the counsellor, but the decision to change must remain that of the partners themselves.

There is one question that I am persistently asked concerning change, 'Supposing my partner refuses to change, what then?' First, none of us can change anyone but ourselves. Secondly, since what my partner is doing is related to what I am doing, I can take the initiative to *change my responses to what they are doing*. I can discover different responses to what my partner is doing which upsets me so much. For instance, instead of allowing myself to accept passively what my partner is doing to me, I can decide to challenge it. By changing my reactions to what my partner is doing to me is to *change the name of the game*. This change of behaviour on my part does at least invite a new awareness in my partner as to just how much their behaviour, or lack of care, is adversely affecting me. Such change of response on my part does, however, need verbal expression, rather than leaving my partner to guess at what is going on. By making new choices I open up the way for improvement in our relationship.

5. Let us look further at this important aspect of *choice*. One of the most persistent complaints of couples in counselling is the feeling of being stuck, having no choice. However much I appreciate that this is what the person feels, I do not believe that this is ever true. Choices can be accompanied by some very unpleasant

consequences, of course, but the choices are nevertheless always there for us to make. Affirming the ability to choose is one of the most effective, permanent and liberating of all the many aspects of counselling. On dozens of occasions, I have experienced the look – a combination of shock, disbelief, bewilderment and amazement – which registers on the face of the person who says to me, 'You mean, I have a choice?' When this idea is firmly planted in a person's mind, the world appears a different place. By making different choices, the world does indeed become a different place for us to live in. Gone are the self-defeating methods of the past, when we allowed others to walk all over us. The power to choose is often accompanied by a renewed sense of self-respect and dignity. Herein lies one of the most important results of counselling, namely the renewal of a person's sense of value and worth.

Choice is a factor which is sometimes overlooked in understanding one's own personal life pattern. More often than not, it is the *abandonment of responsibility* for the choices we make that lies at the heart of our life problems. Many couples start out by denying responsibility for the choices they are, or are not, making. Each time one partner gives in to the other, allows the other to disrupt their happiness, or takes the line of least resistance, choices are being made. I sometimes use a provocative question to get to the heart of this reality. 'How is it you are choosing to let your husband do this to you?' There is usually an astonished look followed by a vehement denial that they are doing anything of the sort. 'It's not my choice,' they say, 'it's just his behaviour that's to blame.' Such is the 'tunnel vision' with which many couples enter counselling, and it is one of the tasks of counselling to correct such impressions. I use the opportunity to explain to the couple that each time they fail to confront a problem, they are choosing not to do so. Unless the couple can be brought to understand the question of choice there is not going to be much progress towards happiness. The temptation, of course, is to resort to blaming, which is really a form of abandonment of our responsibility. After all, if I can persuade you that my unhappiness is all your fault, then it follows that it is your responsibility to make me feel better again. We arrive at an unpalatable truth: *not to confront a problem is to collude with it*. Silence is usually regarded as consent.

Once fresh choices are decided upon, the situation changes. Frequently in marital counselling the issue of sexual responsiveness, or more to the point the lack of it, becomes a central issue. It comes as a shock to some people to discover that the state of affairs can be changed by making alternative choices. As I outlined in *Couples Arguing*, we need to take personal responsibility for what we allow other people to do to us. It takes the same amount of energy to remain silent as to speak out. In my experience, this 'not saying' wreaks more havoc in marriages than speaking one's mind. 'Oh, I couldn't', is a repetitive complaint from weary spouses, and behind it lies another important aspect of what counselling is about.

6. *Regarding oneself as a helpless victim of the other partner* is a distortion often presented in marital counselling. What the complaining spouse does not see is their own strength. For instance, I might remark that they have enough strength to come into counselling in order to remedy their unhappy relationship. I make it a point, while carefully listening to the perceived helplessness of the most downtrodden client, never to believe in it! I will empathize with their pain, and try to enter into the situation they face day by day at home with as much understanding as I can; but I would be making a serious error of judgement if I accepted without further exploration their own sense of powerlessness. *Everyone has power* – it is a matter of what we do with it. What I mean is this: we can either use our power to establish our own position and to defend our rights within the relationship; or we can use our power by *giving it to the other person*. Since this might be a new concept, let me explain what I mean by 'giving away one's power'.

One way we do this is to attribute *exaggerated powerfulness* to another person. This is eventually proved to be a serious distortion of the truth. Of course, we might find ourselves being persuaded by another person that they are more powerful than we are, but we do not have to believe them. What matters is what we are doing with our power – our inherent ability to confront and change things we do not like. If we surrender this ability, we are then surrendering our power to another person, and as a direct consequence we consider ourselves to be weak and helpless – a state of affairs for which we are responsible. In order to change this situation we must choose to take back the power we have attributed to the other person.

I recall one couple who found themselves in the situation described above. A shrinking violet appeared to be mated with a stubborn mule. 'What can I do?' she would ask me, with wringing hands and a hopeless expression. 'Who says he has all the power in your marriage?' I asked one day. She appeared to be puzzled by this line of thought. 'Why – no one,' she replied. Clearly (to me, at any rate) this woman was abandoning her power to her husband, i.e. accepting without question his dominance and her submission. Once she saw the picture from a wider angle (a fundamental aim of all counselling) she began to explore ways of getting a fairer deal out of her marriage. The explosion came, of all places, in a chemist's shop where she had gone to buy a new film for her camera. Her husband began to explain to the woman behind the counter what kind of film his wife required. Almost without thinking, his wife retorted that it was *her* camera, that she was perfectly capable of both buying the film *and* fitting it into her camera, and would he kindly wait outside. To her astonishment, he did just that. She thought, of course, that the Day of Wrath was at hand! It was not. This first occasion on which she asserted herself, and claimed her right not to be treated like a helpless child, proved a turning point in the marriage. Without necessarily changing this 'Me-Tarzan; You-Jane' kind of relationship into one where she became Tarzan, she did at least retrieve the power she had been giving to her husband in allowing him to dominate her for so long. She decided that, on occasions, it was rather nice to have a swing on the rope!

There are many problems like this couple's which emerge in marriage counselling. Human nature being what it is, it seems that one problem merely acts as a cover for another, as yet unperceived, problem. It might, for instance, be interesting to look at the history of this couple's relationship in order to discover how this Tarzan-Jane syndrome began. Was there, for instance, an initial attraction towards the man's strength which afforded, in the early days of their relationship, a solidity and security which she needed? Was there a quality of dependence and helplessness in her which attracted this strong man towards her. In such cases, each is finding in the other a way in which to get their needs met. Their subsequent Tarzan-Jane style of relating merely became a habit from which, long after the original needs had passed, neither could free themselves. It might have been interesting to ask the husband, 'Do you always like playing Tarzan?' It is very hard for strong men to admit that they don't - in case they are thought of as weak or unreliable. (We are confronting at this point the deadly stereotypes in our culture which imprison and paralyze us in our relating to one another.) Of course, wanting him to be Tarzan all the time, the wife could easily place all the responsibility for the marriage on to him. As I outlined in *Couples Arguing*, there are a lot of benefits to be obtained from playing Jane! And it's at this point that a critical decision is to be made: in order to take back the power the wife had been allowing her husband to wield, she must now resume some of the responsibility for both herself and the marriage which had hitherto been considered to be his sole preserve. Many women faced with this implication turn back to the *status quo*. In which case, they are now making a conscious decision to accept their present misery and they will go back to playing Jane in the marriage rather than assert the right to their own power. With this new awareness, it is highly likely that she (at least) will quit counselling altogether, perhaps telling her friends that 'it didn't work!' On the contrary, it worked all too well. Counsellors are not always thanked for removing blinkers!

So we now find that behind complaints like, 'My wife wears the trousers in our house' (i.e. an abandonment of responsibility) lies the real truth, 'I allow my wife to wear the trousers in our house.' It is far nearer the truth to put it this way round. 'My husband is abusing me' translates into 'I'm allowing my husband to abuse me'. This is not to be unsympathetic towards a battered wife, nor is it to condone what this man is doing to her. In counselling, it is the sheer impossibility of squaring the circle that will be revealed. I mean, there is no way that such a woman can have her cake, and eat it. The 'problem' she will present is, 'My husband is abusing me,' with the subsequent misery and feelings of low esteem which usually accompany the battered wife syndrome. However, her real problem is her failure to assert herself, her refusal to confront the man and to take responsibility for what she is allowing him to do to her. Let me illustrate.

It was one of those busy days in the Chicago hospital where I was on-call chaplain. I was bleeped down to the Emergency Room (Casualty) where a battered woman was receiving treatment. She had what appeared to be a pound of raw liver on her face. It was, in fact, what was left of her right eye. Her right arm was broken in three places. A natural sense of outrage emerged within me as I enquired what had happened. Her story was that this happened regularly, that this was her third admission to the E. R. that year, that he must be stopped before he killed her. I agreed. But while I was inwardly furious with him, I was at the same time curious about her. What was she doing with her power? To an averagely intelligent fly on the wall, the obvious answer was for her to leave him, or at least go to the police to have him arrested for common assault. But it was not that simple. It transpired that this woman was one of four 'wives' this man was 'keeping'. He paid the rent on her flat, paid all the bills, and (when he wasn't beating her up) was quite a nice guy. To abandon him or to have him arrested, she would have to take responsibility for her own welfare. She was not willing to do that. Doubtless she went back to being abused. (This kind of behaviour is reminiscent of the story found in Woody Allen's film, *Annie Hall*: a man goes to a psychiatrist, and tells him that his brother thinks he's a chicken. 'Why don't you turn him in?' suggests the doctor. 'I guess I need the eggs,' says the man. It's like that with relationships. We keep going through it because we just need the eggs.) My counselling with this woman could only go so far as to make clear to her what choices she was making, and that she was in fact giving her power away for a free meal ticket! She – at least – thought it was worth it, but I went away sad.

Counselling, therefore, cannot be defined by its results. Counselling is never coercion. It works through *awareness* and *choice*. So I define counselling like this:

> To counsel is to listen and respond helpfully to another person in order to increase their awareness of both their

problem and their inner powers and thus to facilitate appropriate change based on personal choice.

In brief, counselling does not do for you what you can, with some assistance, do for yourself. Rather, it has more to do with deepening your appreciation of your real problems together with their underlying causes. Advice is not a helpful method of approaching problems. It ignores both your resourcefulness and responsiveness and merely reinforces your misconception about your own weakness, and the counsellor's power. Advice also removes responsibility from where it properly belongs: with you and your mate. The aim of counselling, therefore, is to reinforce your coping abilities and your capacity for growth, to rediscover a sense of your own personal worth and value, and to help you to find a more growthful way of dealing with future problems. As you discover a revived sense of your own worth, you will be able to strengthen your relationship with one another, and to share more deeply in each other's joys and happiness.

Counselling is, therefore, life-enhancing in its ultimate aim. It offers hope to those of you who have lost your way on the journey of life, and encourages you to become more fully who you truly are.

2
Major repairs or fine tuning?

Car owners will readily recognize the difference between these two options. Has the vehicle stopped working, and therefore is in need of major mechanical repair, or is it that we are aware that our car isn't giving the performance which we expect? In matrimonial terms, this represents the distinction between a relationship which has ceased to work to the mutual satisfaction of both partners, and one where there are no major problems but they would like a mechanical check-up. Briefly, these two options represent the difference between marital *counselling* and marriage *enrichment*. In the first instance, counselling is appropriate because it is chiefly problem-centred; in the second, a time of mutual reflection can be found helpful to couples who wish to keep their matrimonial 'car' from running into problems. Whereas counselling might be seen as a 'cure', marriage enrichment is seen as 'prevention'. Marriage counselling is indicated when the relationship is basically going wrong; marriage enrichment applies to a relationship which is basically going well, but the couple would like to deepen their understanding and appreciation of one another, and bring fresh resources to improve the quality of their marriage.

My understanding of this important difference is similar to that between ambulances at the bottom of the cliff (counselling) and strengthening fences at the top of the cliff (enrichment). In the past decade or so, all kinds of marriage enrichment programmes have sprung up world-wide. The philosophy is not hard to find. With more and more people running into trouble with their marriages (and the divorce rate which gives the cold, hard evidence of this) it appeared that little or nothing was being done to keep good marriages from going bad. In the medical field, this has been recognized for some time. Whereas for many years the National

Health Service was in reality a National *Sickness* Service (that is, you had to be ill before you qualified for attention), in more recent years all kinds of preventative facilities have become available. The medical profession is now encouraging people to go for various screening tests (cervical smears, blood pressure, cholesterol tests, etc.) as part of a national campaign of preventative medicine. This principle is now being applied to our personal relationships, and a matrimonial 'check-up' can be found of tremendous value to many people today.

Marriage enrichment is usually conducted by means of residential weekends, where the partners work in pairs, so that there is no embarrassing exposure of your intimate relationship with the larger group. Group leaders act as guides and facilitators in order to enrich the quality of each person's life and the love they share together. Many churches arrange special marriage-enrichment weekends as part of their pastoral concern and care, when couples review their relationship; any irritations can be expressed and solutions found. One brochure explains:

> Every now and then we all need to stop what we are doing and take stock of where we find ourselves. We need to examine our lives and directions to find out where we want to go. A Marriage Encounter Weekend offers a couple just such an opportunity.

Many people find such opportunities a valuable experience, when they can strengthen their partnership and learn helpful skills and a greater degree of honesty in order to maximize the enjoyment of their union. (There are some useful addresses at the end of the book for those of you who might be interested in following up this suggestion.) In a further book, I hope to deal at greater length with this issue of how to improve the quality of a basically sound relationship and how it might grow in love and honesty.

3
The counselling process

Is it possible to explain the process by which counselling actually 'works'? If not, then you might do well to suspect the whole enterprise. If we can, then you might have a good idea what you could be letting yourself in for. By 'process' I mean the inner logic and principles upon which counselling is based. While the process will take many forms, such as the different kinds of counselling method and practical application, I believe that there is an inner core common to all schools of thought. What assumptions do I make as I meet a couple in counselling for the first time? While I am attempting to keep an open mind towards them, there are already several factors at work which my training and experience have led me to believe will be of assistance to them.

First, I have a picture in my mind which could resemble their relationship. I think of a kitchen table. At the outset, I know that these two people are going to put certain things 'on the table': grievances, pain, bitterness, resentment, distrust, disillusionment – the catalogue of what they understand to be wrong with them and their relationship. We call this the 'presenting problem'. Their attention will be focused on this 'problem' to which they now seek a 'solution'. I do not for one moment underestimate the degree of pain and unhappiness these two people feel, and I am aware of the risk they are taking in talking about their problems at all. I am also aware of their embarrassment as they select the painful parts of their relationship and place them on the table.

Next, I begin to get curious about what is *not* being put 'on the table'. I make a mental (or, if the first interview, a written) note of what is said and how they view their lives and their relationship. Gradually, I am allowed to enter into their world of broken relationships and unfulfilled dreams, and begin to get a feel of how it might be for them where they find themselves. They have my full attention. But at the same time, I listen with my 'third ear' and observe with my 'third eye' the transaction taking place between us; these additional faculties enable me to monitor what is going on, including my own inner reactions to the story which is beginning to unfold. These faculties remind me of what this couple is *not* talking about or things of which they show no awareness. In other words, people in trouble, couples and individuals, usually display a kind of mental 'tunnel vision'. The truth is being told as far as it goes, but is it the whole truth? Are there bits of life's experience which remain outside their awareness? I almost always find that there are.

So, thirdly, I become actively curious about what might be going on 'underneath the table'. In more psychodynamic language, I get less curious about the *content* of what this couple tell me, and more curious about the *process* of what might be happening between them outside their present awareness. You could think of the content as the top of the table, and the process as what happens underneath the table. The distinction is important, for it represents the difference between what the couple *think* is going on between them, and what is *really* going on between them. Everything that is happening in this couple's relationship is governed by very strict (though for the moment, hidden) psychological rules. It is this hidden area, or what we call the 'hidden agenda', that must be reached before any effective improvements can be made to the way these two people relate.

Fourthly, I try to reach this hidden area by inviting each person to state, as honestly as they can, how they feel. Feelings are a direct route to what lies beneath the table. While problems are always important, they are only important as symptoms of a deeper, underlying problem; for it is only as this deeper problem is uncovered and resolved that any progress can be made towards a happier marriage. Let me give some illustrations of what I mean.

After elaborating on his wife's shortcomings, Fred owned up to his true feelings. 'She's taking me over!' he explained. This is important, not in order to establish whether or not his wife was doing any such thing (the *facts* can wait until later), but as an indication of how Fred is feeling about what his wife is doing.

Feelings take primacy over facts in counselling, which is one reason why counsellors never act as judge or arbitrator. Rather than get into a 'Yes you do' – 'No I don't' encounter, Fred is invited to explore at a greater depth these feelings of being 'taken over'. The role of the counsellor is not to 'take sides' (as many people fear they will) but to act as an *interpreter*, helping Fred and his wife to understand one another better. Once Fred can *own* his feelings, he can abandon the temptation to make his wife responsible for them, leaving her free to respond to his experience of feeling 'taken over'. That kind of deep attention to how he feels lies under the table, and at once gets away from the endless bickering that has been taking place on top of the table. If he feels comfortable enough, Fred might begin to question where such feelings are coming from, and the chances are that he will discover their origins in some early and painful history, prior to his relationship with his wife. Counselling works, not by telling Fred what to do, but by a patient and understanding recognition of how he feels, and by giving him permission to *disconnect* his early experiences from those with his wife. She can now use her energy, not, as previously, in forms of denial and counter-attack, but in a loving awareness of Fred's need to be his own man.

This simple illustration leads us into the essential question as to what actually constitutes a problem in the first place. We have seen that the 'presenting problem' (while often real and painful) is not capable of resolution until the underlying emotional issues are uncovered and expressed. The following story reminds me of one of my own learning experiences, which centred around the riddle, 'When is a problem not a problem?' I finally came up with the answer, 'When it's a solution!' The issue here is not a case of playing with words, but lies somewhere at the heart of what counselling is about. For me, this idea of a solution masquerading as a problem took a long time to register, and was entirely novel. What prevented me from seeing it before was *my own need* to find a solution, a path I should never have gone down in the first place! I have met many people who have been frustrated in their attempts to help others, and no matter what they suggest by way of advice it ends up being rejected, and they feel useless. While the 'solution' appears obvious to the helper, the complainer always finds a way of avoiding or rejecting the help offered. What could possibly lie behind this strong resistance to any form of help offered to them? The answer I finally came up with was, 'Because this person's problem is in fact a solution heavily disguised as a problem!' Therefore, when the helper attempts to remove what appears to be their problem, they are in fact trying to remove their one form of coping with a much deeper problem. You may as well ask a drowning man to throw away his life-belt!

This concept of solutions masquerading as problems helps me as a counsellor in my approach to people in pain. I wondered why no one had told me about it before. Eventually, I found a reference to this strange pattern of behaviour in one of my favourite writers, Sheldon Kopp:

> For example, a patient comes into therapy complaining that he does not get along well with other people; somehow he always says the wrong thing and hurts their feelings. He is really a nice guy, just has this uncontrollable, neurotic problem. What he does *not* want to know is that his 'unconscious hostility' is not his *problem*, it's his *solution*. He is really not a nice guy who wants to be good; he's a bastard who wants to hurt other people while still thinking of himself as a nice guy.[3]

Anna came to see me in a state of high anxiety. She was in the grip of a fear that she might harm her three children in some way. Out of the blue, the thought would enter her head that she would kill her children when she got home, and bath times became a constant nightmare as she tried to ward off these evil ideas. Such obsessional thoughts had been with her for years and no one had been able to solve this problem for her. Reassurances of how much she loved her children and how such an idea was, of course, quite stupid fell on deaf ears. As it happened, Anna came to see me with her husband at a time of wide publicity of child abuse, including a mother who actually *did* drown her children in the bath. I had to ask myself if her children were at risk. Since Anna's irrational fears had been with her for so long, and her children were approaching their teens, I trusted that any real danger had passed. Her love and care for her children were obvious, and everyone held her up as a model mother. What could be the answer to Anna's problem?

Instead of concentrating on the problem which she presented, I decided to look more closely at the *effect* it was having upon her and her family. I asked Anna to tell me what she usually did when these awful thoughts attacked her. Because of the nature of them, those immediate family members and friends in whom she had confided would spring into action. She would call for help. 'What does this "help" usually look like?' I asked her. It boiled down to: (a) getting attention at once; (b) getting someone else to take responsibility for her children; (c) obtaining the company of another adult; and (d) exercising dependence upon another person. This 'help' would be received by: (a) demanding assistance at once; (b) a confessed inability to cope on her own; (c) the manipulation of any helper who might sound reluctant; and (d) an ultimate imposition of her will upon the will of other people.

For argument's sake, let's imagine that Anna's problem is in fact a solution in disguise, masking some deeper need within her, but outside her conscious awareness. I wondered if Anna had a fear of isolation and of responsibility for her children. Was she suffering from a fear of independence and of intimacy with her children? Not that Anna was fooling either herself or other people. Yet I was certain that another fear was lurking beneath the fear she was talking about. Could it possibly be (I asked myself) that beneath her conscious cry, 'My children need protection', was the *un*conscious cry, 'I need protecting!'? Was this hidden fear of Anna's being transferred on to her children? Was it Anna herself who feared being harmed in some way? Did the company of her adult helpers serve to meet *her own needs* rather than the imagined needs of her children? In fact, this is precisely what turned out to be the case when I risked pursuing this line of counselling. It eventually transpired that Anna had a deep, underlying and unrecognized fear of being alone, of not coping with the children, and a fear of responsibility. She had an irrational fear of getting things wrong, which we traced back to her own early childhood. Once we could explore these hitherto unconscious needs and fears, the original fear of harming her children disappeared. What she had been presenting to her helpers as her 'problem' was in fact her 'solution', provided by her own deep and unconscious needs. No wonder her helpers couldn't talk her out of her 'problem', since only through hanging on to it could she get the real need met. They were trying to remove from Anna the one rope to which she clung with such force, and unknowingly they were attempting to take away her only hope or survival. The truth was that, without knowing it, Anna actually had an *investment* in the fear of harming her children, which could only be abandoned once the real problem was unmasked.

Not all those who go into counselling will have the problem Anna had. But it does serve to illustrate the way in which counselling skills can clarify what might otherwise appear to be insoluble problems. The suggestion that people can actually have an investment in their problems will come as a surprise to some people. This is by no means the same as accusing others of enjoying themselves by playing games with their families and helpers. It was Dr Eric Berne who popularized the full implications of *Games People Play* in his best-selling book. He exposed what he called the 'pay-off' principle which lies beneath the problems many people try to solve. By turning the problem upside down, and asking not what the disadvantages are but what *advantages* there are in having this problem, we very often get closer to the truth. This approach is similar to the wise words of Sir William Osler, a noted physician who died in the early part of the twentieth century, who wrote: 'It is more important to know what sort of patient has the disease than to know what sort of disease the patient has.'[4] He was aware that we could become mesmerized or seduced by symptoms while leaving hidden causes unexamined and unexplored. By seeking to find out who she was, and where her presenting problem was coming from, Anna found relief and freedom from what had previously been a destructive life-pattern. Together we could look at this deeper level and the needs which had been hidden for so long, and find for her more constructive ways of dealing with her buried sense of 'getting things right'.

A further (and briefer) story underlines the way counselling can work. A couple came presenting as the main problem in their marriage the very low esteem in which the wife held herself. Joan was continually putting herself down, in spite of the positive and loving way in which her husband tried to affirm her. She just refused to accept any praise or any compliment. She would allow no one to say anything positive about her or her achievements. Constantly, she would compare herself unfavourably with other people. Praise for a well-cooked meal would be met with, 'Oh, no, it's not as good as so-and-so's cooking.' In desperation, the husband persuaded Joan to accompany him to see me. I applied the maxim of Sir William Osler and asked myself, 'What kind of woman has this problem?' and almost at once a new picture began to emerge. It turned out that, in childhood, Joan was in fact very bright, yet this intelligence was ignored by her parents, notably her father. Rather than praise for coming second in her class, he would enquire who came first and then tell her how bad she ought to feel for coming 'only second'. Her marks of 90 per cent were met with, 'And where did you fail this time?' All pride in her achievements and abilities had been systematically destroyed; all confidence in herself had been evaporated under the father's scorching criticism. It seemed to her, as a child, that 'no matter what I do I cannot satisfy father's expectations of me'. More to the point, she received a very positive 'message' that hard work not only attracted criticism but yet more effort. Would it not be better for her to stop trying so hard, to recognize her limitations, and to give up any expectations of receiving praise for what she did. Since, in her father's eyes, her best was not good enough, what was the point in trying so hard to succeed? Over the course of time, her father's implied message of 'You're no good!' was turned inwards and became, 'I'm no good!'

By asking Joan, 'Who taught you that you were no good?' we homed in to the centre of her problem. The problems encountered by her husband, on top of the table, were finding their origins underneath. Once again, behind the *content* of the problem lay the *process* whereby her sense of little worth was being fed by childhood experiences. When she could examine, this time as an adult, her father's attitudes and express her emotions appropriately to such devaluation – much hidden resentment and anger emerged at this point – she began to see that she was carrying within her a belief which did not belong to her but to her father. While she had long ago abandoned any hope of hearing praise from her father, Joan had unknowingly passed this attitude on to her husband, where it did not belong. Slowly she began to restore her lost sense of value, and to relate to her husband not now as a frightened and devalued child, but as a strong and gifted adult. Shadows of father's criticism would of course be there in the background, but she had now found a way of dealing with them when they arose. Her problem (of not allowing any affirmation) turned out to be her solution. By the process of *self*-devaluation she was saving other people the bother of doing it for her!

Here, briefly, is counselling at work. I was not solving problems, still less imposing my bright ideas on an unsuspecting public (the public, as you know, are not quite as unsuspecting as some people imagine!). I was enabling these various people to work out their own solutions to the real problems, and to discover more of the truth about themselves. There was no good advice flying around, of which most of them had had their fill already, merely some common sense backed up by training and experience.

4

The counselling relationship

Couples in counselling enter into a very special kind of relationship with their counsellor. You might be considering whether or not counselling is for you, but you have very natural hesitations, not to say outright panic! Since this is a consumer's guide, you need to know what you would be letting yourself and your partner in for. I want you to imagine that you are a fly on the wall at a typical counselling session in order to get the 'feel' of what, for many of you, might be a completely new experience.

First of all, you see three people sitting down and talking to one another. What has brought them together? As you listen, it appears that the man and the woman sitting next to him are having problems with their marriage. The counsellor is trying to help them sort out their problems. You notice that this 'threesome' has a particular way of relating to each other, and they are concentrating on the subjects brought up by the married couple. The counsellor appears to be doing less of the talking than the other two people, and when they appear flustered or embarrassed, the counsellor simply and naturally asks them to take their time since she realizes this can't be easy for either of them. You, on the wall, begin to wonder why these two people should sit there and pour their hearts out to a person who, moments beforehand, was a perfect stranger. The couple seem to be treating this woman as a friend and confidant; they share their most intimate secrets with her, and they even cry in front of her. You are aware that they are taking enormous risks in telling the counsellor all about themselves and you wonder what the counsellor will do with all this personal information. They seem to be giving out an enormous amount of trust. How can they know it is well-placed?

Something else now attracts your attention as you listen to this small group of people. Only two of them appear to be talking about themselves; the counsellor seems to be an observer and listener, rather than a contributor to the conversation. The counsellor is not saying anything about herself, so you know that no ordinary conversation is taking place. Whatever their roles, you notice that the counsellor seems to play a different role from the couple concerned. How does this relationship differ from ordinary conversational relationships?

It is in the purpose of their meeting that the particular significance is to be found. This is what makes this kind of meeting much more than a cosy chat about non-essentials. While the counsellor will afford the couple a warm and friendly reception, will pay them both careful attention and respect, and will not in any way belittle their reason for coming to see her, there is a peculiar contract which makes this relationship work. You will notice that the counsellor is never surprised or shocked by anything which the two people confide in her. She will receive every statement with due care and attention. She will speak less than the couple themselves. In fact, this is what the counsellor's training has dinned into her – that is, the need for 'non-possessive warmth'. She will neither distance herself so as to appear thoroughly uninterested nor will she smother them like an over-anxious hen with her baby chicks. She is treading a tight-rope between getting too close and getting too far away. Her responses are different from other conversational responses. The counsellor does not intrude into their affairs; she treads carefully knowing that putting their problem into words is not easy for either of these two people. She does not rush into her responses; she allows plenty of time for silences. When the wife starts to cry at one point, the counsellor calmly directs the wife's attention to the box of tissues on the seat beside her, and waits for her to dry her eyes before continuing. This caring attitude seems to draw the couple out more and more, and somehow you realize that there is an unmistakable air of trust in the room. You get the impression that the counsellor cares about this couple, but she shows this not by rushing in with oughts, shoulds, and 'why-don't-you' questions (in fact, you have noticed the counsellor hardly ever starts a question with 'Why?'); rather, you see that something special is going on. The counsellor has created an atmosphere of acceptance and caring concern.

By this time, much of the early awkwardness and embarrassment has disappeared; you can hardly believe that this is the first time these three people have met. They seem to have known each other for ever. Mind you, there have been several moments when things got a bit heated between the two people. When the accusations and blaming really started to fly, the counsellor seemed to be more interested in what each partner was *feeling* rather than *saying* at that particular moment. Somehow, this seemed to get the conversation into a different gear, and the two people started to listen to one another in a new way. You know it was new, because each began to appreciate how the other person felt – and that seemed a new experience for both of them. At one time, the wife tried to get the counsellor to give her advice as to what she should do. The counsellor didn't respond to that request other than by turning to examine the feelings of helplessness which the wife was conveying. Even that intervention seemed to work, for the wife began to tell her story of how she'd always felt unappreciated and inadequate ever since she was a little girl. In some way, this childhood experience seemed to be poisoning the way these two people related to one another; the wife was always feeling pushed around, while the husband always felt he had to take the lead and assume responsibility for everything in the marriage.

At the end of an hour, both partners appeared to have a new and welcome sense of understanding one another, and were eager to fix another appointment when they could take their counselling a stage further. When the husband started to resent the counsellor 'taking sides' with his wife, the counsellor kept cool and did not seem to be affected by this untrue remark. Indeed, she asked the husband what it was she was saying or doing that gave him this idea. It turned out that the husband was unknowingly projecting on to the counsellor the reaction he had always felt in the rows within *his* early family, when, no matter how right he was, his mother would get his father to oppose him. For a moment, he appeared to be accusing the counsellor of behaviour reminiscent of his mother. It seemed strange, didn't it, how both the husband and wife seemed to have so much material unresolved from early childhood memories – long before they ever met – which was still alive and active within their own relationship. Somehow, the counsellor seemed to know this, and was never flustered by it.

But this was no cosy huddle, was it? I mean, the counsellor did not make an easy ride for either of them; she kept them to the point, even when they wanted to get off it or avoid some uncomfortable home-truths. She seemed to be able to confront these two people with what each of them was doing (and not doing) but in a friendly manner, not appearing as an enemy attacking them all the time, but really a friend who cared about them and their relationship. It seemed a new experience for them (and for you on the wall) that someone could have such a concern for truth, while at the same time coming across as basically friendly and open to them both.

The man and the woman went away with hope that their situation was not as desperate, nor as hopeless, as when they first set foot in the room. They each had something to work at, especially the business about being more honest with one another, and not protecting each other from what they both felt. This seemed strange at first, but you noticed that basically they wanted the relationship to work so they would try anything. All the time they had thought they were doing the best for the relationship, they were actually undermining it. This came as a shock for them both, and things began to improve when they took this idea on board. By being less than honest, they had been robbing one another of the chance to put the wrong things right. When the couple wanted to have some guarantees that this sort of counselling would benefit them, the counsellor smiled and told them that she was not responsible for what they would or would not decide to do. 'It'll be up to you, won't it?' she said.

This encounter illustrates how long-term gains are not sacrificed for short-term advantages. Counselling always has in mind not just the immediate problems the couples present, but how they can deal with future problems by a change of attitude or behaviour. This counsellor reinforced the couple's existing strengths and capabilities, emphasizing their power of choice and inviting them to take responsibility for their marriage. By supplying a new model to work with in their relationship, the counsellor was giving them a permanent asset rather than temporary relief which bypassed their main problems. Her role was to model what an honest and open relationship looks (and feels) like in practice, and what kind of decisions they could make towards the improvement of the quality of their marriage.

Another feature of this counselling session was the way in which interest was confined to the agenda of the clients themselves. The counsellor did not allow herself the luxury of bringing her own feelings into this conversation. There will be a time when it would be quite appropriate for the counsellor to express her inner feelings, for instance if either of the partners persistently avoids the issues, wants to change potentially threatening subjects, or is late for appointments. Then the counsellor will not appear to be all sweetness and light! Since she is modelling what an open and truthful relationship might look like, she will confront these various issues directly without attacking the couple concerned. Most of us have no experience whatever of a *caring confrontation* which can work towards a positive alternative to the interminable bickering which often avoids the real issues underneath. Counsellors are not inanimate dupes, nor are they unfeeling robots. They form an integral part of the counselling relationship, and they will fight fairly for their share of it. Most couples in counselling have never witnessed what 'fighting fairly' might look like, and how positive a caring confrontation can be.

What then is the level of emotional involvement allowed to counsellors towards those whom they seek to help? If counsellors are not unfeeling robots, but care deeply for and about those they counsel, how can we describe such feelings? And are they appropriate anyway?

I believe the following words of a psychiatrist, Dr Scott Peck, deserve the careful attention of those couples in counselling (and indeed, their counsellors) who want to know more about the special relationship that counsellors have with their clients:

> There is nothing inappropriate about patients coming to love a therapist who truly listens to them hour after hour in a non-

> judgmental way, who truly accepts them as they probably have never been accepted before, who totally refrains from using them and who has been helpful in alleviating their suffering. Indeed, the essence of the transference in many cases is that which prevents the patient from developing a loving relationship with the therapist, and the cure consists of working through the transference so that the patient can experience a successful love relationship, often for the first time. Similarly, there is nothing at all inappropriate in the feelings of love that a therapist develops for his or her patient when the patient submits to the discipline of psychotherapy, cooperates in the treatment, is willing to learn from the therapist, and successfully begins to grow through the relationship. Intensive psychotherapy in many ways is a process of reparenting. It is no more inappropriate for a psychotherapist to have feelings of love for a patient than it is for a good parent to have feelings of love for a child. To the contrary, it is essential for the therapist to love a patient for the therapy to be successful, and if the therapy does become successful, then the therapeutic relationship will become a mutually loving one. It is inevitable that the therapist will experience loving feelings coincidental with the genuine love he or she has demonstrated toward the patient.[5]

What Dr Peck says here might be questioned by some people, especially counsellors trained in the tradition of regarding any feelings of a client transferred to the therapist as *neurotic*. Clearly, here is one noted therapist who believes just the opposite. To confess genuinely warm and loving feelings to a therapist need not be a threatening experience, except to those counsellors who find close relationships painful to bear. In this case, it is the counsellor who needs help.

In the West, we have become so used to the word 'love' being used as essentially a romantic word, that its use has become an embarrassment for many people. 'Love' and 'sex' appear to be so closely related, if not actually identified (as in sex = 'making love') that the use of the word 'love' is at times unhelpful if not positively suspicious. It is my own practice to use the word 'care' of my relationship with my clients; not that I am afraid of the word 'love' – it's just that I risk being misunderstood less if I use the word 'care' instead. While I know what I mean, I cannot be responsible for what my clients might actually *hear* if I use the word 'love'. The words of Carl Rogers, a noted psychotherapist, come close to how I feel:

> I am very careful not to use the word 'love' because that has so many meanings to so many people on so many different levels that I feel it's more likely to be misunderstood than understood. But yes, I feel the caring that a good facilitator of learning feels for his or her students in the classroom, the caring that a good therapist feels for his or her client, yes, that's a form of love. It's not sexual love, it's not maternal love, it's a very special kind of love.[6]

In case you imagine that even the notion of a therapist 'caring' for you might sound like a cosy huddle, avoiding any confrontation or painful honesty, let me say that, although I am well aware of the danger of caring for couples and clients, I aim at being both caring and confrontational at the same time. For me, the paradox of these apparently contradictory modes of relating is summed up in the New Testament, when Paul writes of the need to 'speak the truth in love' (Ephesians 4:15). Thus, care need not become an interference in the counselling relationship; it can become the atmosphere in which people can learn to love and trust again. The concept of the late Dr Carl Rogers of 'non-possessive warmth' gets the balance about right for me. It means neither an antiseptic distancing from the couple and their problems, nor an intrusive over-anxiety which stifles and clings. In the light of the traditional psychoanalytic attitude which avoids any close relationship with clients, I reproduce from a prominent psychoanalyst some words which allow an approach to the client which includes care (on both sides) and which does not have to be viewed as neurotic:

> Freud's recommendation of emotional aloofness and coldness, like a surgeon 'who puts aside all his own feelings, including that of human sympathy, and concentrates his mind on one single purpose, that of performing the operation as

> skillfully as possible', sets an ideal which analysts, for a time, strove to achieve. Later, of course, it was realized that the analyst must not only be this surgeon, but he must also be the warm, human, friendly helpful physician. He must be both. Freud's advice to analysts on the role of warmth and sympathy in the analytic process is rarely quoted in full. True, he urged restraint; but he also urged tact and eschewed cold rejection of his patient's confessions of their love for him. He advised against both ignoring 'the transference love' and responding to it. Only in this context can the patient's con ditions for loving come to light.[7]

These words of Dr Karl Menninger remind us of the struggle within those of us who counsel others when we attempt to be *both* caring and objective at the same time. The counsellor's sense of objectivity is essential if the counselling process is to be profitable from both points of view – that of the couple and also the counsellor. This is the so-called 'therapeutic alliance' and it might at first sight appear strange to you. For one thing, it is a temporary relationship, not a permanent one. Secondly, it is unequal in the sense that the focus of attention does not include the counsellor but is totally on the couple themselves. Thirdly, there is a very strong sense of a 'contract' between the parties involving expectations on both sides which are clearly spelt out at the beginning of the counselling process. But should the counsellor be free to bring his or her own material and experience into this counselling relationship? I must confess that in my early days of counselling, I tended to go 'by the book' and keep my own experiences of growth and pain to myself. I recall the first occasion I decided to risk sharing my experiences with a client who seemed to me to be struggling with what I once struggled with. That moment of honest sharing, when we met as two wounded pilgrims together, proved to be the turning point in her own journey into wholeness and joy. So, I nail my flag to the mast, and as usual Sheldon Kopp puts it neatly:

> When I work with a patient, not only will I be hearing his tale, but I shall be telling him mine as well. If we are to get anywhere, we must come to know one another. One of the

> luxuries of being a psychotherapist is that it helps to keep you honest. It's a bit like remaining in treatment all of your life. It helps me to remain committed to telling and retelling my tale for the remainder of that pilgrimage which is my life. Research into self-disclosure supports my own experience that the personal openness of the guru facilitates and invites the increased openness of the pilgrim.[8]

While it is true that some counsellors can appear to be either stand-offish and distant or easily led into an overly protective role – none of us gets the proportion of 'distance-closeness' right all the time – most counsellors will opt for a caring approach, with all its inherent dangers, rather than a cold and clinical approach as if the counsellor were sitting behind a perspex screen. I call this 'creative distancing'. If the truth of Aesop's fable is to be believed, it is the warmth of the sun rather than the cold north wind that ultimately facilitates uncovering and disclosure.

But how long will this counselling relationship last? Will you and your partner be expected to stay in counselling for ever?

5
How long will it take?

I remember a man coming to see me one day in a very deep depression. His wife felt worried by his strange behaviour which was a reaction to a recent redundancy. He sat through our first meeting like a small schoolboy and it was obvious that this reactive depression was serious and possibly demanded long-term psychotherapy. When I reached for my diary to make another appointment, he asked me if he needed to come again! I was, of course, flattered that he thought I could work wonders in sixty minutes, but I decided to correct his fantasies.

There are usually no instant solutions to long-term problems. The duration of counselling is so dependent upon the unique needs of the couple in counselling that we might as well ask, 'How long is a piece of string?' No one can give that kind of 'guesstimate' at the commencement of counselling. There are simply too many variables.

When issues of *cost* are involved, there might be just so much money to spare, and that factor might determine the duration. Some counselling agencies, like RELATE, operate on a basis of the ability to pay rather than the fixed rate that some counsellors charge. Any difficulties regarding the funding of counselling should be discussed with the counsellor at the beginning, because this might determine the frequency of the counselling sessions. Usually a fortnightly appointment, rather than a weekly one, eases the financial strain on the family budget. As the counselling progresses, it is then possible to lengthen the time between appointments as the immediate crisis recedes. Counselling is never allowed to wander on and on aimlessly.

The nature of the problem of the couple concerned will also determine how long they need professional help. Most counsellors have had the experience of seeing couples only once, since the initial risk of seeking help from outside can so stimulate communication between the two people that they are able to sort out their own troubles as they begin talking to one another again. The acknowledgement that help is in fact needed if the relationship is to be salvaged can itself be a healing experience. Also, it could take an appointment with a professional counsellor to bring home to a reluctant partner just how seriously their husband or wife views their situation. Even if only one of the partners comes for counselling, this is in itself a very strong signal to the other partner that all is not well in the matrimonial camp. My own view is that if one of the partners in a marriage is unhappy, then the *marriage* is unhappy, and that danger signal ought not to be disregarded. However, in most cases, counselling proceeds over an undetermined length of time, and when I am pressed to answer the question, 'How long?' I reply, 'I have no idea, but let's see how far we get in, say, half a dozen sessions.' There has to be some realistic period during which the couple and the counsellor can assess their progress, and this can be agreed upon by the people concerned. It is often found that, as we have noticed earlier, the problems people present at the beginning of counselling prove not to be the real problem at all, and this naturally takes time to emerge. Like all healing processes, counselling involves time to grow into more healthy behaviour patterns. Most of us cannot change the habits of a lifetime overnight.

No counsellor is going to expect either an individual or couple to conform to a set of preconceived ideas concerning how quickly their situations are going to change for the better. You and your partner will be treated with respect for your personal individuality; as with all good tailoring, you won't be expected to fit into 'off-the-peg' solutions. Your programme of counselling will be 'made to measure' according to your needs.

Finally, on this important question of time, if you are having serious problems with your relationship I would urge you to seek help sooner rather than later. I understand the temptation to stick your head in the matrimonial sand and hope the difficulties will simply go away. Counsellors (like doctors) often think, or say, 'If only you'd come sooner!' I have seen many couples disappointed with the counselling process because they left things far too late for any repairs to be done to a marriage where the damage was irreversible. Some couples appear to have their bags already packed (frequently with another person waiting in the wings) and then seek the help of a counsellor as a last resort! Frankly, this rarely works. There is a point beyond which help is impossible. The hurt and pain is just too deep, and the relationship is already dead. Counsellors are not into raising the dead. But what if it is not too late, and the wounded relationship can be healed? How will the changes you and your partner decide upon affect your future relationship?

6
The two faces of change

Thousands of couples have discovered a new lease of life for their marriages following a period of counselling. Old ways of relating which only led to misery and desperation, have been replaced by new and creative life-styles. A fresh chapter has been entered into through the changes the couple decided upon. Joy and happiness have become the norm, rather than the pain and unhappiness which used to prevail. For such couples, change has meant a new lease of marital life. But there is another side to change which you would do well to consider before opting for marital counselling.

Change can have an unwelcome and threatening side to it, and some people find any proposed change (even if they are desperately unhappy) profoundly disturbing. I usually refer to this, perhaps surprising, possibility at the outset so that couples are aware of what they are entering into. This risk is particularly relevant where only one partner is seeking help.

Relationships are often like pieces of delicate machinery: changing one part will affect the whole. Investigating one part or aspect of a marriage might open up other issues which might not be so welcome. As we have seen, some people want to have their cake and eat it. While she sees the 'problem' as his offensive drinking habits, he might respond by saying that he only drinks because of her ongoing affair with the milkman. Now a different picture emerges. As we say in counselling, 'Everything's related.' *She* wants his drinking put right, but without any attention being paid to what *he* wants. When *he* insists she gives up the milkman, she might insist he takes more responsibility for the sexual side of their relationship. This is what I call the 'peeling the onion' syndrome. It is my continual experience that, whatever the 'presenting problem' might be, we usually end up somewhere else.

One problem seems to hide behind another, perhaps deeper, one. Such deep penetration into our inner selves can pose a serious threat to most of us.

In counselling you just can't have it both ways. Symptoms are related to causes and, as we noted earlier, the 'content' of an unhappy relationship is directly related to an underlying 'process'. You can't change one without changing the other. This Janus-like nature of change draws our attention to the two sides of putting things right in our relationships. You can't have the gain without the pain. Counselling is not about whitewashing over serious problems, any more than medicine is. It is no good painting the house if the foundations are falling to bits. Frankly, some people come into counselling thinking in terms of 'magic wands', but the truth is otherwise. Sheldon Kopp is quite right when he speaks of some people who 'prefer the security of known misery to the misery of unfamiliar insecurity'.[9] I think of one couple who illustrate this kind of reaction to the full implications of counselling.

It was the wife who first came to see me. She brought a catalogue of complaints against her husband. He was making her life a misery and, in spite of all her efforts, there was no visible improvement in the marital situation. She felt she had come to the end of the road in terms of her own efforts; unless he changed his behaviour she saw no future for the marriage. Her perception was that her own shortcomings in the marriage were due directly to his impossible behaviour. We entered the familiar world of 'if only'. *If only* he would be more loving, kind, considerate, understanding, compassionate, etc. her world would be wonderful. It all sounded reasonable, *too* reasonable to be credible. I asked whether or not her husband would like to accompany her to one of our sessions, and he agreed to do so. As you can imagine, a totally different picture then emerged from the one she had painted. When *his* catalogue of complaints about *her* shortcomings was mentioned, she became profoundly disturbed. Her double messages (saying one thing but meaning another) were paralyzing him; if he came too close, he was 'smothering' her; if he kept his distance, he was being 'uncaring'. If he offered help, he was 'interfering'; if he didn't, he was 'indifferent' to her needs. He was in a 'no-win' situation, and thus chose drink and depression as his escape from this impossible situation.

When we reached the issue of what *changes* he would like to see in the marriage, she visibly panicked. She saw no relation between what she was doing to her husband, and the misery of which she complained. Her perception (actually, a *misperception*) was that 'it was all his fault'. Counselling is not about attributing blame to either side; it aims at getting under the table of the relationship, to the mechanics of how they relate to each other, and what changes they can mutually decide upon to improve the quality of their lives. On this occasion, the implications that the wife as well as the husband needed a change in behaviour, became far too uncomfortable for her to continue with counselling. She swept out in high dudgeon, complaining to me that 'counselling didn't seem to be doing me any good'. I never saw them again. I placed their file away with mixed feelings. While recognizing how difficult change can be for some people, this couple represented the *two faces of change* – one welcome, the other not. She wanted *him* to be changed while not being willing to face the implications of any change in her own life. Presumably, this woman was going to find it easier to put up with his behaviour than to change her own. Of course, the husband could have found out how to alter his own responses to his wife's behaviour rather than resort to drink and depression. But putting up with his behaviour proved, in this instance, to be far less threatening to the wife than changing her own behaviour patterns.

Did counselling 'work' for this couple? At one level, of course it did not. Since nothing changed in the way these two unhappy people were relating, they presumably went back to the *status quo*, preferring their known misery to the unknown terrors of a full-blooded examination of their negative relational techniques. In terms of not giving the wife what she wanted, counselling 'failed'. Doubtless, this woman will entertain the fantasy that she had 'tried' marriage counselling, 'but it did no good'! Actually, the truth is otherwise. She had not, in fact, 'tried' counselling: she had manifestly *avoided* it in terms of what counselling would mean for her. Since counselling is never about 'success' or 'failure', it is not possible for counselling to fail. It might prove too threatening in its implications, or the counsellor might be incompetent. It might be more or less helpful to couples, but since it never sets out to 'succeed' in the first place, it cannot be said to fail.* At one level, this woman's counselling sessions proved to be *too* successful for her liking, in bringing home to her the responsibility which she carried as well as her husband. Unless responsibility is accepted by both partners and worked through in all its painful implications, no outside help will change things. If a person's hopes are unrealistic to begin with, the expectations they hold are doomed before you start. Even counsellors cannot square circles!

* See the John Rowan quotation on page 53.

7
The outcome

We noted above that counselling is never intended to last forever. Couples will either tend to 'cop-out' from the full implications of changing their lives, or they will decide to make adjustments which give them both a greater degree of peace and fulfilment. Either way, is there life after counselling?

The short answer is, 'It all depends on what the couples *do* with their counselling experience.' Since we are all individuals and therefore unique, what might 'work' for one couple might not work for another. Each couple is a special 'mix', even though some problems seem to appear regularly. Human life crises are no respecter of persons, but each couple will view their own particular crisis through their individual lenses. Indeed, what might be seen as an urgent crisis by one couple will be regarded as a storm in a tea-cup by their next-door neighbours.

Let us assume that a couple have been to see a counsellor with a marital problem, and over a period of time their problem has been fully aired, each partner has had their say, and they come away wiser for the experience. They know more about how the other person feels, and have explored their own inner depths of feelings as well. They have some direction as to their future together. What next? First, responsibility for the way they choose to relate to one another is entirely their own. Marital problems usually concern the behaviour pattern of one of the partners which the other one finds unacceptable. In counselling, the aggrieved partner will have levelled with their spouse concerning what it is that upsets them so much and has been the cause of their distress. This need not mean that the 'fault' is that of the spouse at all. It could be the aggrieved partner's reactions that were entirely inappropriate. For instance, I remember a woman coming to see me who complained about her husband 'ogling' any woman on television, especially if she had an ample bosom. The 'Miss World' competitions were subsequently banned by the wife, who used to censor all TV-viewing that involved sexy women. She really wanted to change her husband's behaviour and wanted me to tell her how to do it. She was convinced that something was wrong with her husband's sexual appetite. What could she do to correct this fault in her husband?

I risked asking her how she felt about *her* breasts. She burst into tears, and poured out a long history of chronic feelings of inferiority which she had focused upon her own breasts. She was ashamed of them, and longed to look like the women she envied on TV. (Feelings of inferiority, by the way, are usually transferred on to some *bodily* part; in men, it is usually the size of their penis.) What started as the husband's unnatural sexual appetite, turned out to be the wife's own feelings of inferiority, feelings which persisted in spite of her husband's frequent reassurance that he was quite satisfied with her physical appearance. All this fell on deaf ears. The real need was not for the husband to change, as she had originally supposed, but for her to learn how to accept and love her own body and to receive the affirmation her husband was giving to her. After counselling, they had to go back home and work out the problem between them. While he needed to be sensitive to his wife's need for encouragement and affection, she needed to be less touchy about her body and learn self-acceptance. The husband could then give up his mistaken sense of guilt for having caused his wife's problem, and she could begin to accept the love he offered. While he could now abandon responsibility for his wife's feelings of inferiority, he needed to deepen his appreciation of how she felt about herself. She needed to take responsibility for carrying childhood images of herself as the family ugly duckling into her adult relationship where it was manifestly untrue.

What was the counsellor's role in all this? Since counselling is not about coercion, responsibility for the outcome of this couple's crisis remained solidly with them. The counselling skills are there to enlighten, to reveal, to challenge and confront; they are also there in a caring attitude which is deeply committed to the understanding of what was going on in the lives of these two people in terms of their own personal pain and unhappiness. Within the openness and trust of the counselling relationship, this couple could examine their fears and fantasies, in the presence of a person who would not be shocked by their story, and would not take sides. The counsellor remains impartial. But counselling is one thing; what people *do* with counselling is quite another. The counsellor's responsibility does not extend beyond the counselling session. He is in no way responsible for what the couple chooses to do with material discussed between them. Even if, in the extreme circumstances of a couple subsequently deciding to separate and divorce, the counselling process cannot be held responsible. Marital counselling is neither directed towards the maintenance of a shaky relationship nor towards the separation of the two people concerned. That separation happens sometimes is, of course, quite true. Some couples who are subsequently divorced have had some form of marital counselling. Unfortunately, some people seek counselling as the last resort, when the rifts have run too deep to heal. Such wounds are often found to be beyond the reach of the healing process of counselling. Does this mean that therapy has failed? Some would see it this way, but this is to misunderstand the counselling process from the beginning.

Summary to Part 1

When couples come for counselling, it should be made clear that:
1. The counsellor is not committed to the maintenance of their marriage at all costs.
2. Nor is the counsellor committed to their separation.
3. The counsellor *is* committed to the side of truth and integrity, and to the possibility of healing, love and growth *within* their existing relationship.
4. Counselling is about an honest analysis of existing problems and the choices which might exist for the couple in order to regain a happy way of relating, fulfilling to both parties.

As a counsellor, I feel a sense of sadness when people decide that change is too costly for them to contemplate. They either go back to their life of misery and unhappiness, or they decide they must part. I believe couples have the right to choose such alternatives, but I am not responsible for their choice. I am – and must allow myself to remain – open to the pain of other people; but if I cross the line into assuming responsibility for their lives, I am no longer a counsellor but a rescuer working out his own pathetic script on people who happen to be making choices I might disagree with. Of course, counsellors do not always hear the end of the stories of couples they counsel. Some simply stop coming and we never know what happens to them. Sometimes I hear that so-and-so have parted; I also hear of the transformation of some relationships. Just as I take no blame for the former, neither do I feel I can take any credit for the latter. Naturally, I want to be open to the affirmation that others might give, but I must watch my human pride so that it does not get out of control. I feel the sense of privilege in being for some people a light-bearer and darkness-scatterer, and that somehow through the counselling process I have facilitated creative change in their lives. Yet I also want to affirm to those who change unhappy lives into happy ones that is it ultimately *through their own choice* that such changes have come about. That is work I cannot do, nor can any counsellor. Knowing this, my hope is that the couple have now found a way of dealing with conflict more creatively so that they can approach future problems, which will almost certainly arise, in a more constructive way.

Couples in counselling, therefore, stand at a cross-road in their lives. They come seeking improvement in their relationship, for resolution of seemingly intractable difficulties, and a new quality for their relationships. The way ahead might lead to a painful uncovering of issues hardly thought of as important, but which lead on to hidden factors which, like peeling an onion, lead on to others. The counsellor is the guide in this process; he or she knows that there will be strong resistance and avoidance to confront before any progress can be seen. This will mean uncovering the fear, embarrassment, guilt and resentment underneath, like allowing the pus to be squeezed out of a boil. Such a process of healing will hurt, especially our pride, but the cliché is a true one: *there is no gain without pain*. The couples are in pain anyway, but most of that pain is what I call destructive pain, like pushing a splinter down into your finger in the hope that it will go away. But it will also hurt getting it out!

Merely by coming into counselling you cannot ensure a magic wand will be waved, and all will be well. True, some couples approach counselling in the nature of a small child who cries, 'My world is broken, and you must mend it!' No counsellor can do this. The best we can offer is to try and help you find out *why* it is broken in the first place, and to examine the effects of this brokenness in your relationship.

If the break is irreparable, and what the modern divorce procedures now call 'irretrievably broken down', does this mean that counselling is a waste of time and money? Personally, I don't think so. I believe this not because there are no incompetent or clumsy counsellors; far from it. We are, after all, merely human and fallible. I believe that, when couples separate after counselling, the process has not failed, since we're not playing winners and losers. John Rowan sees

> two very seductive traps for the therapist – being right and being successful . . . every time I want to be successful I am secretly working for self-aggrandisement, striding to the far shores of my profession on the stepping stones of my clients. Success and failure are both largely illusion; people develop in quite a wavy and contradictory way, and what is success on one level may often be failure on another level. It is really a mistake to use the words 'good' and 'bad' at all; every failure is a success, and every advantage is a disadvantage. All a client really needs is someone who is prepared to stay with them while they explore the darkest and most difficult parts of their experience.[10]

Counselling, therefore, is not about 'right' and 'wrong', 'good' or 'bad'; it is about being more or less helpful, more or less honest, more or less relevant. The counsellor may very well fail to love, or understand, or empathize with a couple. But this is not to attribute failure to the whole process which the couple and the counsellor together undertake.

On those occasions when two people discover, in the course of their counselling, that their marriage is over and they would be happier living apart, the counsellor can still have a valuable role to play. He or she can help to make that separation process more creative by allowing the couple to find a constructive way of ending their relationship and of saying goodbye to one another, free from the bitterness and recriminations with which many matrimonial break-ups are littered.

For, in the nature of things, the counsellors and therapists are but *transitional* figures in the lives of couples. Crisis, pain or ordinary human unhappiness brings them together for a while. They talk, explore, try to pretend to one another; we all defend and play our roles. In the end, it sometimes happens that people grow and change for the better. They drop pain-producing behaviour patterns and find a new way to love, a new way to *live* again. They find freedom to *be* who they are, and to rejoice in their own uniqueness and earthiness. In that process, everyone grows – the counsellor not least of all. For he or she, too, is a pilgrim on the journey through life; there is no immunity from human pain for the counsellor!

In the final analysis of the counselling process, we will all discover, as Sheldon Kopp rightly says, 'No one is any bigger than anyone else. There are no mothers or fathers for grown-ups, only sisters and brothers.'[11]

PART 2: WHO NEEDS COUNSELLING?

Instead of spending so much of my life trying to fight off depression, overcome anxiety, and deny inadequacy, I can willingly experience just how sad and scared and helpless I sometimes feel.

8
Couples

The couples in the title of this book cover a wide variety of situations, and can apply to any two people in any social relationship. Couples include the married and the unmarried, as well as those who live together in a homosexual 'marriage'. Couples represents a term which is intended to be inclusive rather than exclusive. The moralists might huff and puff about it, but the fact cannot be escaped: people are choosing to live together outside the legal confines of marriage, and on an increasingly large scale. Many such people are, no doubt, children of divorced or separated parents and were themselves part of the pain and heart-ache of the break up of *their* parents' marriage. Today's couples are often children of yesterday's marital mayhem, and they cannot be blamed for not wanting to rush into marriage when they found their parents in full flight to get out of it. In addition, the social benefits available to one-parent families are such that 'shot-gun' weddings are almost a thing of the past, in spite of the rising rate of illegitimate births (nearly one in five). It is often because the younger generation value marriage as an institution so highly that they are not willing to rush headlong into it. Moralistic bullying is not going to change their thinking. The people who choose to live together rather than marry officially are not voting against marriage. On the contrary, they are mostly in favour of marriage at the right time and to the right person. Meanwhile, living together has almost become a modern rite of passage for young people emerging from puberty. Thousands of people form part of the divorce explosion, especially following the relaxation and reform of divorce laws in 1971 and 1984, and it ill becomes the older generation to teach the children caught up in the painful results of separation and divorce how to suck matrimonial eggs!

When we come to consider the issue of counselling couples together a new reality emerges. Counselling two people at once is a different task from one-to-one counselling, since a couple is a greater reality than the sum of the two parts of the individuals concerned. In this threesome (the couple and the counsellor) each is relating to two other people at the same time; in terms of group dynamics, three people represent much more than merely 2 + 1. For example, using a triangle ABC

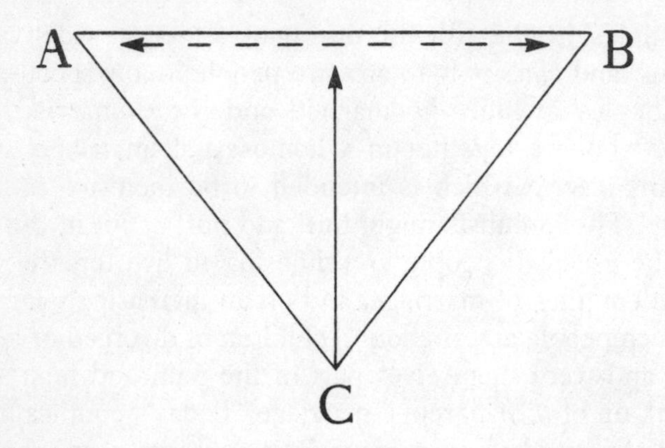

let A and B represent the couple, and C the counsellor. While each person is aware of the other two, a new reality begins to emerge such as what is going on between A and B, A and C, and B and C. The counsellor becomes aware not just of the husband and the wife, but also of what is going on between them, (represented by the dotted line which joins them in the diagram). The counsellor's task, therefore, is to manage two sets of feelings, assumptions, expectations and anxieties (including his own) *at the same time*, while remaining impartial and fair to both parties. The 'coupling' process, therefore, introduces another element into our experience, namely, 'the relationship'. It can be thought of as similar to the invisible 'bonding' process of a newly-born infant to its mother. When such bonding is either absent or mismanaged, we realize the inherent dangers this can pose for the deprived child. This is also true of the lack of bonding in marriages, and it is from damaged relationships that the need arises for couples counselling.

And there are plenty of damaged relationships around – perhaps yours? The pessimists are not slow to tell us why this should be:

> For example, marriage has to serve the needs of individuals who live longer than before, are less supported by the extended family than their forbears, have more opportunities to meet other partners because of social and geographical mobility and are less tied by moral and social constraints than was the case a hundred years ago. They live in a culture where religious affiliations have grown weaker, one governed by materialist values which can suggest that relationships as well as objects may be disposable. Moreover, there are expectations of marriage to provide personal happiness and fulfilment, even to make up for less than fulfilling relationships in the past.[12]

Out of our own background and upbringing, we bring to our adult relationships an inherited history of the way we relate to others. We bring our own perceptions (or misperceptions) concerning who we are, and who we believe others to be. For, as John Donne reminded us long ago, none of us is an island; we are all part of a family history, a society, a race, a culture. We therefore bring to our marriages our own understanding of what personal relationships are, and ought to be. Most of us simply take on board the way our own family related to their inner and outer worlds: our inner world is that which exists within the boundaries of what we call 'family', while the outer world concerns the way we treat those outside it. The rules for such relating can be (and often are) totally contradictory. While there can be fierce loyalty to members of our family, we can be entirely ruthless to those outside it. Take, for example, the Boswell family in Carla Lane's *Bread* (BBC1). While honesty and loyalty rule inside that family, there are no such rules applied within the DHSS office. Although we may trust members of our family, there is no guarantee that we will treat others outside it in this way.

Attitudes like these act as a backcloth when we begin an important intimate relationship. We will inevitably bring into that relationship the way our background has taught us to relate, either with openness and honesty, or with doubt and suspicion. Even our reactions *against* our family background are affected by our family traditions. If our past relationships have been, on the whole, creative and rewarding and relatively free of pain, we will be free to form attachments without too much trouble. If, however, past relationships – getting close to significant others – have been the cause of deep hurt and pain, we will proceed more cautiously, placing the important person on a kind of 'emotional probation'. 'Boy meets girl', therefore, has more in it than meets the eye. Couples are complex realities.

In the animal kingdom, of course, mating – or what the in-jargon calls 'pair-bonding' – is a common enough experience. Such mating is based on sexual and procreative needs – after all, Mother Nature is no fool! We call this, in human relationships, 'falling in love'. He or She becomes special. What kind of experience is this? One writer describes it like this:

> When a person falls in love what he or she certainly feels is 'I love him' or 'I love her'. But two problems are immediately apparent. The first is that the experience of falling in love is specifically a sex-linked erotic experience . . . We fall in love only when we are consciously or unconsciously sexually motivated. The second problem is that the experience of falling in love is invariably temporary. No matter whom we fall in love with, we sooner or later fall out of love if the relationship continues long enough. This is not to say that we invariably cease loving the person with whom we fell in love. But it is to say that the feeling of ecstatic lovingness that characterizes the experience of falling in love always passes. The honeymoon always ends.[13]

Thus, if Dr Scott Peck is right in his assessment, many couples – in our Western culture, almost all – come together based on this notion of 'falling in love', which turns out to be not only sexual in its prime motivation but also temporary in its duration. Neither of these factors is a firm base for marriage, or indeed any long-lasting relationship. Unless the initial attraction can be used to start a journey together in which both people can grow in awareness of, and in a greater commitment to, the value of themselves and their partner, the relationship is likely to be of short duration. These two unique individuals who now form the 'couple' are held together by 'the relationship'. If the original attraction is sexual, as Dr Peck suggests, then it is essential to pay attention to the on-going relationship *after* this initial attraction has faded into the background.

Naturally, sexual attraction and relationship are very much connected. One woman says, 'Speaking for myself, when things are going well in my relationship with my husband, the sex is good. When they're not, the sex is awful. It's as simple as that.' Another woman says, 'The relationship is everything. My husband doesn't need a book on how to make love. He needs a book on how to make a relationship.'[14]

As I sit in my consulting room listening to people discussing their problems, most of them have to do with broken relationships. What set out as a mutual attraction turns into animosity and bitterness. Love can turn to hate. What was once an inability to tolerate the lover's *absence* turns into not being able to tolerate their *presence*. Many such relationships bear witness that there is truth in Dr Peck's pessimistic view of falling in love. Once the honeymoon is over, what then? Where can we find healthy models for a more creative way of growing in the relationship we have chosen? On what principles might a good and growing relationship be based? If we can find for ourselves a working norm we might begin to understand the problems that can occur in intimate relationships and prevent their occurrence. What models are on offer?

9
Models of partnership

Let's begin with a simple illustration from our understanding of the motor car. It is a piece of sophisticated machinery, governed by some important rules. In order to get a good and reliable performance out of it, and to prevent break-downs at inconvenient moments, these rules must be observed. The car, for instance, needs regular servicing; it needs a change of oil now and then, new oil-filters, water, petrol, anti-freeze, and regular M.O.T. check-ups on its lighting, steering, brakes, etc. The car has become so much part of our lives that we hardly bother to think about these needs. We take them for granted and we know the price we pay when we neglect to give our car the mechanical attention it needs. We do not need an AA man to tell us that many break-downs could have been avoided if only we had paid a little more attention to the basic rules of care and maintenance.

Although a marriage relationship is not an inanimate object like a car, nevertheless I believe that similar rules apply. *Relationships need regular servicing if we are to get the best performance out of them.* Why on earth do we assume that our most important and intimate relationships are in some way self-vitalizing and self-sufficient without any further action on our part? Many couples who are fastidious in the care and maintenance of their car have a total blind-spot when it comes to the 'mechanics' and 'maintenance' of their relationship.

I spoke to a husband recently using this model. I made the bland assumption that he would never think of running his car into the ground and replacing it with another. How mistaken I was! 'That's just where you're wrong,' he told me. 'I never do a thing to my car, and in fact I always run it into the ground, and only when it packs up do I pay it any attention. I usually replace it anyway.' Stirred but not shaken, I responded by asking him whether or not he thought there might be any connection between the way he treated his cars and the way he treated his wives – he was at the end of his second marriage. Was there a similarity? On further discussion, it transpired that his attitudes towards his cars and his wives were strangely parallel: he assumed everything to be OK until smoke was pouring out from under the bonnet. Well, on this occasion there was plenty of smoke pouring out of his wife's bonnet. She left a month later.

I once discovered a similar assumption, accidentally, in a man who had invited me to his home for dinner. His wife had cooked a truly splendid meal, and afterward I told my hostess how much I appreciated it. I was unprepared for her reaction. Suddenly, she swung round to her husband. 'You see! Tony appreciated my cooking. You've never paid me a compliment like that in all our married life!' Without a trace of concern, the husband replied, 'Look; you can assume your cooking's OK until I tell you otherwise.' Again, the assumption was there that, like the other husband's car, everything was to be considered OK until something went wrong. There was no input, no affirmation, no regular 'servicing' by expressions of appreciation and love. No wonder both relationships had serious problems.

If we push this similarity between cars and relationships a little further, we find another truth. This concerns the sharp contrast in the way in which problems are approached. How is it we think it is both natural and sensible to take our car to the garage for servicing and repair, while at the same time considering taking our broken relationship into counselling as a sign of weakness or disgrace? I have never yet heard anyone, taking a car in for a service or repair, saying to the mechanic: 'I feel so ashamed, so guilty, for having to bring my car to you; I feel I'm letting my family down by asking for your help. If my husband knew I was here, he'd kill me!' Why then do we feel guilt or shame for coming for professional help regarding the breakdown of our most important relationships? Of course, many people feel they *ought* to be able to sort out their own problems – which is a bit like saying that you *ought* to be able to strip down your engine and do your own car maintenance yourself. Some people can do their own repairs and servicing, but most of us cannot. So, if it is no sign of failure or disgrace to seek professional help from your car mechanic, why does it have to be a sign of failure if you consult a marriage guidance counsellor or other form of help? I regularly hear clients telling me of the blame they receive from other members of their families for consulting a counsellor. They feel it is a blot on the family escutcheon. While free to wash their dirty car in public, people are not allowed to express the concern for their marriage in the confidential atmosphere of a counselling session without this becoming 'washing your dirty linen in public'. That is quite simply a double standard, based on fear, suspicion and ignorance.

While there may be some help in this mechanical parallel to marriage counselling, it is quite obviously deficient in at least one particular. It is too mechanistic, for personal relationships are capable of *growth and development*. I need to supplement this model, therefore, with one which implies these important elements in human relationships. Whereas a car is a collection of material things, a living relationship can actually die.

Plants, in our homes and gardens, need watering and nourishing if they are to thrive and give of their best, and flourish to their full potential. The same is true of human relationships. If the environment is unfavourable, they will die. On their death certificate will be: 'Cause of death: severe and longstanding neglect.' This verdict could be written on many Decrees Absolute. More time, attention and money is often expended on the family pets than on our marriage partners. The belief – assumption, maybe – seems to be that our partners are self-vitalizing and self-sufficient. It should not be surprising to anyone that, starving for love and affection within a moribund marriage, and suffering from psychological rickets due to lack of emotional vitamins, desperate people respond to warmth and affirmation coming from outside their marriage. Critical observers may vent their disapproval on such 'unfaithfulness', but to many people this is a matter of life and death. One man said, 'If I'd stayed in that bloody marriage, I'd have died! I only discovered my self-respect once I'd taken the risk to get out.' But, just as marriages can die, they are also capable of growth and development – like our plants. Some people tell us that talking to our plants can actually make quite a difference to them. Good communication is at the heart of all healthy and developing relationships.

Some people acquire an *un*healthy model upon which they base their understanding of marriage. It might help to clarify what I mean by giving you some examples. (Is yours among them?)

The 'Siamese Twins' marriage

Siamese twins are one of the saddest outcomes of a pregnancy. They are joined together, and the process of separating them demands a very skilful operation which can sometimes succeed, but often involves the death of one of the twins. I am using this phenomenon to describe, graphically, how it sometimes happens that two people become glued to one another in a relationship, two bodies but only a single thought between them. Take the hilarious example of Howard and Hilda in *Ever Decreasing Circles* (BBC1). They both have the same inane grin on their faces, and – just to make the point – often turn out in identical sweaters. They appear to agree on everything, give way to each other on everything, and speaking to one of them is like speaking to the other. Don't be deceived into thinking that, because we laugh at them, there are no marriages like this. If they are a caricature of a marriage, remember that a caricature does not invent the situation: it merely *exaggerates* it. Howard and Hilda will never need counselling – until, that is, one of them decides to become a real, separate individual. At this point, their marriage will face a real crisis. Like separating real Siamese twins, the counselling operation is always delicate and unpredictable.

The 'Doll's House' marriage

There are a number of emphases in this model of a relationship. It gets its title from the characters in Henrik Ibsen's play, *A Doll's House*, in which the couple represent the stereotyped male and female roles of the late-nineteenth century. The husband was brought up to be strong and independent while the woman was raised to be emotionally dependent on her husband. But the plot reveals how dependent the husband actually is on his wife, although she keeps this from him in order to preserve his male ego. While the husband unwittingly drives his wife into a kind of slavery, he still retains his concept of her as the weak one; in fact, she has all the power, though choosing to pretend otherwise in order to protect him from the real truth.

'Doll's house' marriages, therefore, are based on a kind of confidence trick. The wife uses her power in order to support her husband's need to be in control of the relationship. She protects her husband from the unpalatable truth that he needs looking after. The only way in which the husband can receive such emotional support is to become ill; because when you're ill even big, strong men need to be looked after, while he can entertain the illusion that it's his illness being looked after, not him. Neat?

A variant is 'Mothers and Fathers' lived out in the real world as if they were both children playing with a real doll's house. Everything has to be 'nice' and 'neat'; everyone plays the game, never rocks the boat, and naturally is always pleasant. There are no rows, no problems, and each is falling over backwards to be nice and accommodating to the needs of the other. There is no assertion of individuality; the couple merely mirror one another and take their cue from the reflection of themselves.

'Peter Pan and Wendy' marriages

Peter Pan was the charming little boy who never grew up. Much has been written about this syndrome in recent years, partly because it has emerged as an unhealthy phenomenon in the exploration of hundreds of marriages in counselling, and in part because of the Feminist Movement's influence in uncovering the effect this sort of marriage has had on 'Wendy-wife'. In brief, 'Peter Pan and Wendy' marriages are ones in which the wife dominates, only because the husband won't. 'Wendy/Wife' will come across as 'wearing the trousers', and 'Peter Pan/Husband' as the typical 'hen-pecked husband'.

These 'little boy and mummy' types of marriages have, of course, their appeal. While each partner keeps to the rules, all will be well. But when one changes, or matures, or simply gets to the end of their tether (and it's usually 'Wendy/Wife' who reaches this first), the fat is in the fire. In Barrie's play, it is Wendy who is the first to leave Never-Never-Land. In the Broadway musical, based on the play, Peter Pan sings:

> I won't grow up.
> I don't want to go to school
> Just to learn to be a parrot, and recite a silly rule
> . . . I won't grow up.
> Let's be quiet as a mouse and build a lovely little house for Wendy. . . . she's come to stay, and be our mother, at last we have a mother,
> She'll be our mother, it's nice to have a mother,
> Wendy, Wendy, stay.[15]

It is a long and hard journey for Peter Pan/Husband to get out of Never-Never-Land; for it entails relinquishing his childish life-style, his chronic dependence upon his wife, and his fear of growing up. Counselling could help this couple to expose the basis of their relationship, and work towards a more adult base on which to build their future relationship.

As you consider some of these unhealthy styles of relating, you may have been thinking of what has gone wrong in your own relationship. Not all problems are capable of inclusion in such neat categories as I have suggested above. But it is important to point out the signs which indicate that help is needed in a failing marriage.

My own rule of thumb is this: *When one partner is unhappy, the relationship is unhappy*. If one partner has a problem, then the relationship (which includes that partner) also has a problem. It makes no difference if *one* of the partners is happy with the way things are, and sees no problems at all. The relationship, we noticed, is that invisible bond of love and trust between two people, like the third side of a triangle. It is this 'coupling' which can become weak and sick and, without care and attention, can die. The need for help is indicated when the partner experiencing the problem discovers that they can make no progress with their loved one. They have made all the allowances, they have tried patience and understanding, and they seem to have given their all. In the end, they draw a blank. The pain and unhappiness gets too much to cope with, and they decide, perhaps at someone else's suggestion, to find some help from outside.

Counselling is also indicated when problems cannot be resolved, and when they seem to recur every time there is a row. If you find yourself still fighting over the same things you were fighting about last year, and the year before that, then some kind of outside help is probably called for. If important matters are not getting resolved, but merely come up again every time you quarrel, the cause is probably some deep-seated matter of which neither partner is aware. The issue might be, for instance, loss of trust, or dishonesty, or you might be playing some of the marital games I wrote about in *Couples Arguing*. Either way, this kind of quarrelling is an indication that you are not going to solve this problem on your own.

Now it is one thing to know and accept that help is needed with your relationship; it is quite another to go out and get it. In our British culture we have inherited some very strong resistances to counselling, so we may as well confront them at this point.

10
Some barriers to counselling

The question of feelings

Behind some of the protests concerning 'going public' with family problems we can discern the question of sharing deeply held, yet deeply suppressed, *feelings*. Men, in particular, do not find this aspect of marriage counselling very comfortable, since somehow or other our culture has maintained the impression that emotions are the sole preserve of the female sex. Since most men, by the way, are brought up by at least one woman, it is hard to see why this phenomenon is carried on through successive generations. As a matter of fact, big boys *do* cry! (Did the woman who told me, in front of her desperately depressed husband, 'I can't be doing with weak men,' give the game away?)

In a remarkably frank and helpful book, *Why Can't Men Open Up?*, the authors draw attention to the special difficulties men have in getting in touch with their feelings, and how they differ in this respect from women:

> Why do men insist on keeping an emotional distance while women plead for intimacy and support? How different are the emotional needs of men and women?
>
> It is possible to overstate the differences, certainly. Not all women are open, nor are all men closed. Yet men and women, in general, do have different ways of expressing their emotional needs. Where many men try to guard their feelings or deny them, many women share them eagerly; where many men tend to hold themselves at a safe distance from the emotions of others, many women tend to give emotional support as readily as they accept it. To feel truly fulfilled, a

> person must both give and receive and many men are equipped to do neither. 'In affairs of the heart,' one psychologist told us, 'men and women often speak different languages.'[16]

Thus, some men find it incredibly threatening to have to sit and listen to their wives or partners expressing their feelings to another person. If they were at home, as likely as not they would simply walk out of the room in order to avoid such emotional honesty. Tears and other ways of expressing strong feelings are sometimes written off by men as, 'Now you're just being emotional!' It so happens that 'being emotional' is part and parcel of being *human*, and indeed more relationships founder through *lack* of the expression of honest feelings than through their appropriate display. On other occasions, of course, it is the angry husband who is feared by the wife. Anger is a powerful emotion and certainly not the monopoly of men. Some couples go to extraordinary lengths to avoid displaying anger. There may be plenty of *indirect* anger flying around – burnt toast, slamming doors, glares across the Shredded Wheat – but most of it hardly ever gets expressed directly. In almost every case of marital counselling I have been involved with, strongly held feelings manage to find expression in the relative safety of a counselling session which the couple feel they could never have shown in private. Somehow, the accepting and non-judgemental presence of the counsellor makes it safer to say what has been bottled up for years. At least the initial responses to such feelings can be invited and shared in the presence of the counsellor, whatever more private debriefing takes place in the car on the way home.

When deep feelings are being suppressed, or an emotional issue is obviously being avoided, the counsellor can invite the couple to express these feelings directly to one another. 'How would you like to respond to what Jim has just said?' is an invitation to Jim's wife to be honest and open towards him. Here, the counsellor acts as a kind of monitor or mirror to the couple (rather than, as might be feared, as a 'peeping-Tom') as s/he tries to facilitate the communication between them. It is not surprising, therefore, that people erect barriers against counselling. Such emotional honesty may be both foreign and threatening to some of us, and yet the open acknowledgement and expression of our feelings can work towards improvement in the quality of our relationships. There are others, of course, who sigh with relief when, after years of denial, they can finally come clean and let go of their feelings. They are included in what I call, 'Things-I've-always-wanted-to-tell-you,-but-was-too-scared-to-say!'

Oughts and shoulds

Another familiar barrier to counselling is the firmly held belief that somehow or other we *ought* to be able to cope. 'We *shouldn't* need anyone else to tell us what to do!' some couples say. Asking for help of any kind is, for many people, an extremely hard thing to do. It seems to strike at the very heart of our imagined powers of coping or ability to solve our own problems. To reach a boundary beyond which we seem unable to go in helping ourselves, is somehow regarded as an admission of defeat, and that is a hard pill to swallow. So our personal list of oughts and shoulds reveal our levels of expectation concerning how we manage our lives. Many families are brought up on the script, 'We sort out our own problems; we don't take them outside', and that makes it harder for some of us to 'break the family rules'. There was a fairly typical example of this attitude in an episode of the TV soap-opera, *East-Enders*, when the character Arthur was suffering from a nervous breakdown. The family tried everything to keep him at home (and 'out of the loony bin', said his wife) long after the point when outside help was an urgent necessity. However strong Arthur's family was – and it is a strong family unit – there came a time when comfort and sympathy were simply not enough.

Of course no one wants to encourage the frame of mind that cries for help every time there's an emotional twinge, like a crowd of helplessly inadequate hypochondriacs. We do need to develop helping resources within our own families, and this is what many people are doing without any fuss or bother. Many families have some parental, or grand-parental, wisdom figure to whom they bring their problems and, truth to tell, have often found sound guidance and advice from such sources. Many minor problems in marriage relationships are dealt with in that way, and the resources of wisdom in one's family need to be emphasized and explored. We certainly do not need to despise such sources of strength and assistance. However, for example, GPs sometimes find that they have to refer their patients to a specialist consultant for their professional opinion and advice, and they do this without any sense of shame or guilt. That referral process is not a mark of weakness or inability in the doctor; on the contrary, it is part of his or her strength, and indeed care for the patient, to refer them to more expert hands. No one can be expected to know everything. If we were to think of the counsellor as a kind of 'emotional AA man', to be called out when our matrimonial car runs into mechanical trouble, perhaps we would be bringing counselling into the realm of what is considered normal and natural, rather than foreign and alien to our way of life.

There are many people who find themselves in relationships where they feel it is their lot to suffer. 'I've made my bed, I ought to lie on it,' they say. Or, 'I ought not to complain. Edgar does have his good points.' They continue in their marriage, in Thoreau's chilling phrase, to 'lead lives of quiet desperation'. A man told me, 'I'm being glued together at the moment by anti-depressants.' Some of us find it incredibly hard to seek help, because it is through our 'oughts and shoulds' that we have held together our image of our ideal self. No one finds it easy to let that go. The fact that many of those expectations are completely irrational doesn't seem to register with some people.

And then, underneath the question of feelings and our oughts and shoulds, we find a deeper barrier –

Fear

This is a very basic yet understandable barrier to any form of self-disclosure. What might come out in the counselling process? Will everything have to be laid out in front of a stranger? One thing is certain: whatever we fear may come out into the light, whether we are conscious of it or not, is having some effect upon our relationship with our partner. It takes a great deal of emotional energy to *conceal* our inner truth and our feelings, energy which is vitally needed for the well-being of that relationship but which, through concealment, is not available to it. A choice might have to be made whether or not to risk letting something out of the matrimonial bag and to be willing to face the consequences of doing so. Very often in personal relationships, it is not the fact of the matter which disturbs the other person when we tell them, but rather that we have *concealed* how we have been feeling for so long. In, say, the case of a sexual affair it sometimes happens that it is the fact that one person has deceived the other by silence and concealment that hurts most and may be potentially more threatening to the continuation of the relationship than the affair itself. Partners often enquire, 'Why didn't you tell me . . . ?' in utter disbelief and shock. When material such as this emerges in counselling it enables both parties to come to terms with their fears and begin to explore them more freely.

The barrier of fear is a strong one, and can have a long history of pain behind it. Maybe we have good reason for not being honest about our misdemeanours, because such honesty was severely punished when we were children. Fears of what counselling will 'do' to people are widespread, and frequently groundless. Nevertheless, such expressions of fear need to be heard patiently and sympathetically. It is to be hoped that, through books such as this, the process of counselling will appear less threatening to those who need the kind of help it can bring, but are afraid to make the first move. I usually assure my clients that nothing is going to happen to them without their consent. Even when fear prevents a person from talking about the problem directly (for instance, sex) then it is possible to explore that person's feelings concerning the subject, without going into painful details which that person is not yet ready to explore. I sometimes ask, 'What do you think would happen if you spoke about your problems regarding sex?' They might reply, 'I'd feel dirty and ashamed.' Without prying into the no-go area of sex, their feelings of shame might more profitably be explored, especially regarding the history behind such an association of 'dirt' and 'shame' with 'sex'. To face and overcome the barrier of fear is a major step forward in that person's growth, and of course to the growth of the marriage. One thing is certain; no one is going to consider you 'silly' or 'stupid' for being afraid.

Pride

This is closely connected with our personal 'oughts and shoulds' and our fear barrier. Pride comes out in many forms. For example, one woman who told me, 'I never thought I'd come to this' – as if seeing a counsellor was somehow next door to the debtor's prison! I think of the man who told me, 'I'm not having anyone else telling me how to run my marriage,' and he seemed taken aback when I happened to agree with him. It is all too easy to use a *misconception* about the nature of counselling as an excuse for not taking part in it. Even so, coming to share apparently insoluble problems with another person can be a blow to our personal pride. A woman said to me that she felt ashamed at her depression following the death of her husband, since she was not in the class of 'those people who cannot cope for themselves'. Needing help desperately during such a crisis in her life, she became her own worst enemy by not asking for it sooner. Her barrier of pride would not allow her to do this, until sheer desperation overcame it.

But there is no reason for shame in recognizing, and owning, our personal limitations; that's a lesson I had to learn in coming to terms with my own limitations, especially as a professional helper. I felt deeply for the doctor who came into my consulting room one day, flopped down in the chair, and let out the most tragic and eerie moaning I have every heard; he sounded like a wounded animal, and in a way he was. 'Do you realize', he asked me, 'how hard it is for one helper to come to another helper for help?' I said I did, for I felt precisely like that when I first entered therapy to unravel my own problems. I, too, had to face, and overcome, my own barrier of pride. Equally, I meet with spouses whose main problem concerns the pride of their partners in not coming for help. Like those coping with sick partners who won't go to the doctor, there is often a feeling of guilt in betraying their husband or wife when they reach the end of their resources.

Ideally, of course, marriage counselling is entered into together as a couple, but there can be a significant change in the marriage effected by just one of the partners coming for counselling. The pride of the resistant partner does not have to represent an insuperable barrier to the improvement of the relationship. Indeed, it is often the case that, seeing the pain and desperation in their partner, the proud person can overcome their inhibitions regarding counselling. However, this is not always the case. One partner may stubbornly refuse to admit a problem as a means of covering up their own fears or pride. What then?

The counselling task will centre around the expression and acknowledgement of the feelings of the person who has decided to seek help. Frustrations can be ventilated, their sense of helplessness expressed, and their inner pain uncovered. When such feelings are not being expressed directly to the absent spouse, it can be of great benefit to be able to do so within the acceptance and non-judgemental atmosphere of the counselling process. Different responses can be explored towards the other partner, and the power of choice can be reinforced along the lines I suggested on pp. 15-17.

Cost

What about the cost of counselling?

One of the encouraging signs within the National Health Service is the seriousness with which counselling is now being taken. There are counselling and psychotherapy facilities now available at some general hospitals; and although there is the danger of a fresh association between counselling and 'illness' because of the association with 'hospital', which is regrettable, nevertheless these free facilities are to be welcomed. The bad news is that the supply is outstripped by the demand in some places (at least, there are long waiting-lists in those hospitals I know). So free counselling is becoming available, even if you have to wait for it. There are also some local counselling agencies which do not work on a fixed fee per session, but on an agreement with each couple based on what they can afford to pay. For instance, RELATE has no fixed rates, and you do not have to pay for counselling. However, they hope contributions will be made to the costs of the work, and this is usually discussed with couples by the counsellor.

Other counsellors work in private practice and this does involve the payment of fees. Most of them have fixed hourly rates, but others operate a sliding-scale depending on the couple's circumstances. The financial commitment to counselling needs to be carefully considered at the outset. Some people feel guilty about 'spending money on myself', and this attitude could be usefully explored by the couple and the counsellor together. In the case of my own paid therapy, I reached a point when I considered that I could not afford *not* to find the money somehow. It was hard to do this on a clergy stipend, but in a way I found that the commitment to paid therapy was in reality a commitment to my own worth (what Americans call 'voting for yourself') and this proved to be an important aspect of my own therapy. Paying for counselling also calls into question the issue of the priorities of the couple concerned. How high does expenditure on the improvement of the quality of your happiness together come in your budget?

Paying for counselling might seem like a luxury to some people, and it is a matter not to be taken lightly; it will prove, in the end, to be a question about the family's system of values and priorities. Let me stress, however, that there are voluntary agencies available, including RELATE, where the lack of funds need not prevent counselling. There may also be other counselling centres in your area, and your local information office, public library or Citizen's Advice Bureau, will supply details. (I have put a few national agencies at the end of this book for your information.)

Summary to Part 2

I have considered a few of the most familiar resistances to going into counselling: our feelings, our ideals, our fear, our pride, and the important matter of cost. Perhaps your own barrier is not among these? *Time*, for instance, is often thought to prevent counselling but, to be honest, we usually find the time for what we want to do, and it is a matter of personal priorities as to what we value most. At least you are now aware how your in-built reservations about counselling can be hidden behind what appears to be a reasonable objection.

So, who needs counselling? It is open to all who wish to be able to talk over matters which concern them and their marriage in a non-critical, accepting atmosphere with a sympathetic and trained listener. You will not be treated as incompetent twits, nor thought of as wasting anyone's time. No problem will be thought of as unimportant or, as many people tell me, 'making a fuss about nothing'. You will be treated with respect and understanding and will be expected to take full responsibility for the outcome of the counselling process. You will not be patronized (nor matronized), but treated like anyone else in pain and distress. You will receive a patient hearing of your problems and will be invited to share quite honestly and openly what it is that is troubling you.

We can now turn to the kind of areas in human experience from which many of the problems found in marriage counselling arise.

PART 3:

WHAT PROBLEMS DO PEOPLE BRING TO COUNSELLING?

If no one knows me, who can love me?

11
Me and my shadow

When it comes to sorting out the problems posed by inter-personal relationships, it is a Golden Rule that we need to begin by looking at ourselves. Mind you, it's not where most of us want to begin; we've already made up our minds who the real villain is, and we have our guns loaded and pointed at our partner. We might have fired off the odd round or two already in the matrimonial mayhem. We're totally sure that our partner is in the wrong – or is at least 90 per cent of the problem! When you go to a counsellor, therefore, you may be surprised and annoyed, to find that he or she is hardly interested in putting your partner straight. The counsellor will, however, help you to take a long, hard look at yourself. You may be surprised at what you find.

Neither you nor I arrived in this world a fully-fledged adult; like the rest of nature, we came up through a process of growth and development, and in a very specific human environment. No person's upbringing is perfect or ideal, nor would we expect it to be, as those of us who are parents readily recognize. Since we are not perfect, neither will our parenting be. The best we can hope for is that the treatment of our children will be 'good enough' (to use Donald Winnicott's helpful phrase). Even in very large families, we are all 'one-offs', individual and unique. This family context, however, was our early training ground and the place where we learned what being human means. To the extent that this early model had its faults, it was inevitable that we should have inherited them. So each of us carries the results of our upbringing: my perception of myself and others; my beliefs and doubts; my hopes and fears; my attitudes towards feelings; and of course my dreams. We may call this early upbringing our 'conditioning'; it comprises the ways we have been taught to believe and behave, our list of 'oughts' and 'ought nots' and our inherited way of dealing with crises. Be it noted here, that there is a great deal of nurturing included in this conditioning process.

Adolescence is the period in our personal development when we have the opportunity of making some adjustments to this emotional, intellectual and moral luggage which we have carried since our childhood. It is often a time for rebellion, for kicking over the traces of those aspects of our parenting which we no longer care to take with us into our future. It is a time for making up our own minds on certain matters: our religious or political belief system; our moral principles concerning what is right and wrong; and, above all, our own sense of personal identity. The chief task of the adolescent phase is to arrive at an answer to the fundamental question, 'Who am I?'

This emerging sense of Self, of course, has two very important limitations: first, there is no such thing as *total* self-knowledge; and second, selfhood is a growing, changing reality.

The first limitation reminds us that, according to most psychologists, our consciousness represents about 10 per cent of who we really are. Our awareness extends only to the tip of a large personal ice-berg: about 90 per cent remains below water. We'll see the implications of this fact, in terms of personal relationships, a little later on. The second limitation is that there is no *real* me, a solid and unchanging reality. We are, as human beings, more accurately to be thought of as a continuing *process* rather than a *product*. It is better to think of yourself as 'becoming' you. Again, looked at this way, our lives are much more open to growth and change than ever we could have imagined. But it is this very aptitude to change that presents couples with most of the problems they will face in their relationship. When one says to another, 'You're not the man/woman I married,' I usually interpret this as a compliment; for if I were the same person as I was twenty years ago, something would have gone drastically wrong with my developmental process. Remember: you are a process, not a product.

Now, back to where Boy meets Girl. Two *emerging selves* come together, two changing realities, who for a moment in time recognize the attraction each feels towards the other. The tips of two icebergs begin an elaborate ritual of separation from other icebergs in the sea of life, and finally decide to unite. While they are aware of the attraction of what lies above the water, they might not be so aware that they are also accepting the 90 per cent that lies beneath. Let me now drop the analogy, and return to the implications of this factor in terms of human relationships. It is out of that 90 per cent, or what we can call 'the unconscious' that our shadow-self emerges. All the bits of ourselves which we have, over the years, either denied or suppressed because they did not fit in with our self-image, remain buried – but buried alive! Incidentally, a great deal of what is good and healthy can also find itself buried deep outside our awareness if, during our childhood, we were taught that certain acts or attitudes did not comply with family norms. In making the Herculean effort to please mummy and daddy, and find acceptance by others, we would (as children) have suppressed almost any of our good and natural attributes in order to obtain this goal. Many problems which we experience later in life often find their origins here, not least where these concern our natural expression of sexuality.

Whatever the particular problem, therefore, that drives you to seek help in your marriage, the chances are that sooner or later something from your shadow-self is going to emerge. It would be easier to think of two people as actually four: two apparent selves, plus two shadow-selves. Even though, in the church wedding service, each of you may have pledged, 'All that I am I give to you,' you might not have understood the full implications of what you were saying. You each take on the *whole* of who the other person is, not just the bits you happen to like and find attractive. Marriage is a kind of package deal; you can't expect to take the part you like and reject the rest. So the fact that I am a changing individual, on the one hand, and possess a considerable shadow-self, on the other, means that human relationships are always going to be volatile and fraught with danger. The trick of a successful marriage is not to be frightened by these truths, but make them both work for you and your partner, to your mutual satisfaction. The best relationships are those where growth and change are not seen as essentially bad and threatening, but good and welcome.

There can be no doubting the implications of these facts of

human personality as they bear upon the way we relate to one another. Men and women certainly do not need to be 'tissue-typed' prior to marriage. In fact, the very differences between couples – their background, family norms, and age – can be a positive help in their future relationship. If we possess a flexibility by which we can cope with such differences, there is no reason why such unions should not succeed. When couples can be helped to realize that they are both *in the process of becoming themselves* and also that they are *not totally who they appear to be*, a different picture emerges into their conscious awareness. From these two basic psychological truths comes the background against which their current problems and disagreements can be more profitably examined. As a potential consumer of marriage counselling you need to be aware of this.

I have a poster in my consulting room which reads:

> The truth will set you free,
> but first it will make you miserable.

This has been not only my own personal experience in therapy, but also that of hundreds of people I have counselled over the past thirty years or so. As I was helped to discover more about Me and my Shadow, quite frankly it hurt. I did not like the journey into my inner reality, and the discovery of pain and hurt that had lain dormant there for years. I also felt threatened by the fact that I was 'becoming' me; it made me feel insecure. Yet while these truths were making me feel miserable, they were also the means whereby *I was being set free* from the crippling effect of my past. To acknowledge that I was a changing, not a static reality, both threatened *and excited me;* to discover the hidden and suppressed side of my personality both appalled *and exhilarated me.* The excitement came as I recognized my potential for changing into a self more consistent with who I felt I wanted to be; and the exhilaration came when I discovered that there was not only shame in my shadow but also an untapped potential for self-acceptance and self-fulfilment as the old masks of pretence and conditioning were peeled off. Of course there were risks as I came to implement these truths within a personal relationship which had been static for years; but not for one moment did the pain involved ever make me consider the enterprise to be anything but worth while.

It is precisely at this stage, when you are beginning to get in touch with the submerged part of your self, and your need to break out of old, outdated patterns of behaviour and thought, that there is the possibility of a crisis in your relationship with your partner. *There is as much possibility for growth and enrichment in that process as there is potential danger for the relationship.*

A husband came to see me complaining that he felt depressed. He was a man in his mid-thirties, with his own business, an affluent life-style and a devoted wife. There were, it seemed, no circumstantial reasons for his depression. But he did not like the 'What's the point?' attitude he felt towards life. However, as we explored his own personal background, his wife's opinions were coming more and more to the fore, and I suggested to the husband that if his wife would like to accompany him to one of our sessions, she would be most welcome. It might even help her to explore how she felt about his being depressed. An interesting picture began to emerge. She complained of his almost total lack of feeling *anything*. Their habitual way of relating was one in which she took responsibility for the quality of the marriage; she was the active one, he the passive partner. What would become of this way of relating should he get through his depression and become more active in the marriage? How would she cope with a fully-feeling husband? As the counselling proceeded, the wife began to feel threatened and, as the husband's shadow-self was explored, she began to wonder what would happen to their relationship. Counselling is certainly no easy option, therefore, and provides no simple, off-the-peg solutions.

On the theme of personal identity, I recall a wife who illustrates how her past conditioning had solved one problem only by creating another. She was a vivacious woman in her late thirties who complained about experiencing a paralyzing anxiety which was having a bad effect on her marriage and other social relationships. She had a totally disarming smile, even when describing painful feelings. Somehow, that smile seemed strangely at odds with her story, and I risked sharing my awareness with her. Without dropping the smile a fraction, she replied, 'People only like you when you smile'. I asked her where she had learned that, and she told me it came direct from her parents. Later, she told me how frightened she was when she had lost control at a party during an anxiety attack, and had to leave in a hurry. I asked her what frightened her about losing control, and her immediate reply was (still smiling), 'You must never lose control'. Again, I enquired who had taught her that and, of course, she said, 'My parents.' In order to gain the approval of her parents when young, she had to keep to the parental 'do's and don'ts', but lost herself in the process. So, talking to this woman was like talking to her mother! Slowly we unpacked the other material which she had learned so thoroughly at her parents' knees, and only then did she fully realize how much her *present* was being governed and determined by her *past*.

These two illustrations lead us to another important area from where interpersonal problems arise in marriage counselling.

12
The unfinished business of my past

As we have already seen, experiences in our childhood, which caused much pain or humiliation, tend to get buried (alive) in each of us. Most of us can remember situations in which we were quite powerless to prevent physical or sexual abuse happening to us, for as a child we were weak and entirely vulnerable. Others were too powerful for our infantile resources to challenge. We simply had to take what was handed out to us, while at the same time perhaps gritting our teeth and promising (silently) to get even with them one day. Such experiences become part of the hidden element in our own personal 'iceberg'.

One man I met had suffered a great deal of pain and humiliation due primarily to his illegitimacy, and this led to a severe deficiency in his view of himself and his value. He had, in fact, a basic mistrust of life and people, and he had erected an effective barrier against himself and his world. This sort of barrier is formed quite spontaneously in childhood; it is part of the self-protective mechanism with which we are all born, a gift from Mother Nature. A gift – yet at the same time a burden, since we now distrust, not just those people who hurt us in the past, but everyone *without distinction*. So the belief is born within us that 'you can't trust people', people in general that is; they are *all*, without exception, potential exploiters and likely to put us down as 'they' did in the past.

This man, like most of us, had some kind of unfinished business from his past, which was affecting the way he viewed his world and himself. No wonder there were problems in his marriage. Such a lack of basic trust, from one standpoint, was entirely understandable; he had been hurt too much ever to enter into a trustful relationship again. The pain simply ran too deep. But, while that original pain was now buried in the past, it was still operating within his marriage. For in marrying he had been motivated by another part of himself which yearned for love, affection and companionship. Such a man usually attracts the kind of woman who feels that she has enough love for both of them and is hopeful of winning him over in time. In this case, time ran out. She gave up trying. It was like trying to love a brick wall, and even love has its limits. This couple brought to marriage counselling the problems of a wife who was running out of patience and a man who, while not wishing to lose her, was scared out of his wits to take down his brick wall in case he got hurt again.

Another couple had been bickering and fighting for many months, always about the same list of things: money, criticism, not enough love, etc. I asked the husband how he had felt about himself as a child, and he remembered that, no matter what he did for his mother, it was never good enough. He was always criticized. He received a very strong 'not good enough' script from his mother, and having picked up a very negative image of himself as a child, it was hard for him to drop this image in his marriage. So his 'I don't like me' script, picked up from his mother, was being put upon his wife and came out as, 'You don't like me'. It turned out that there were many people around him who, he thought, did not like him: her family, his family, mates at work. His basic inability to accept himself was being turned into an imagined rejection by other people. When I asked him what happened to him when he allowed people to get too close to him, he said, 'They always end up hurting you'. This was a line from his earliest childhood memory, a very painful one for him, yet one which was still operating in the marriage and turning it into a nightmare for them both. Here was some of his unfinished business from his past, still haunting and hurting him, even though the events themselves occurred years ago. He needed to recognize that his wife was *not* his mother, and that he could approach her on an entirely different basis. It would be taking a risk to do this, but there was no other way forward than by letting go of the past and relating to his wife on the basis of the here-and-now reality of her love for him. This did not, nor could it, guarantee that she would never hurt him, but at least it would be as an adult, not a helpless and vulnerable child. Counselling would be aimed at increasing this man's awareness of his *adult* coping abilities. (For this man, and others, the next chapter would be of crucial interest.)

Here are two illustrations of how things which happened to us in the dim and distant past can go on affecting (and *in*fecting) present relationships. They form the basis of many problems met in marriage counselling. Barriers erected against what might have been tyrannical attacks – verbal and physical – when we were young, remain intact in a relationship where they manifestly do not belong. Such defensive behaviour in the past enabled us to emerge from such experiences having survived the ordeal, but with damage to our earlier ability to be open and sensitive to the world around us. Part of us is now blocked off, even from our own awareness, so we are unaware of anything being amiss. We simply come to recognize our damaged personality as 'me'. These suppressed memories, however, still go on operating like some hidden electronic eye which can detect an intruder into our inner and outer space at a hundred metres. Our barriers automatically come into effect, shutting off people just as they did when danger approached in the person of father or mother or whoever it was who terrified us when we were young. Such automatic responses are now out of our conscious control, and we come up with such phrases as, 'I don't know why I'm doing it – I don't want to hurt my partner, but I find that this is what happens.'

This curious behaviour is one of the sure signs that help is needed to unravel what is actually going on in such a person's mind. Clearly some unconscious, reflexive material is at work. Such automatic defensive barriers effectively block out the other person, whereas they were originally designed to block out a childhood experience now long past. Failure to distinguish between, say, 'father' and 'wife' means that it is now impossible for anyone to approach us either physically or emotionally. As our partner feels shut out from us, deep problems of intimacy arise, in effect for us both, but usually first for the partner who is being unconsciously rejected. Unfinished business from the past always plays havoc with our present situation.

Similar difficulties arise for some husbands when they feel shut out or rejected by their wives. Especially is this experienced when physical closeness and sexual advances are attempted. The tension of the body, tightness round the mouth and eyes, and an interior withdrawal away from the very touch of the partner are all signs that this woman carries with her some unconscious hurt. Her inner electronic eye warns her of the approach and the shutting-off mechanisms are automatically activated. The approaching husband feels this coldness, which might express a range of feelings from mild distaste of sex to a positive revulsion. Frigidity, that is, sexual unresponsiveness in women who feel no erotic sensation, causes a great deal of difficulty in personal relationships. It is not a case of the woman not loving her husband; often it's quite the reverse. She does love him and needs him to love her, but the body is giving out such strong messages that it over-rides her conscious wishes. There are important, psychological forces at work in these patterns of behaviour, the full treatment of which might require professional psycho-sexual counselling.

The outcome of such behaviour will inevitably mean that we are operating within our *present* relationships from a pattern based on *past* experiences. There is a need, therefore, for us to find ways by which we can get the past out of our present. In the helpful phrase of William Bridges, for many people their present is merely a past they have not yet let go of.[17] An interesting illustration of this pattern occurred to me recently.

A couple had got themselves locked into a strange pattern of behaviour which had become uncomfortable for them both. Whenever she got home from work, which was usually later than her husband, she would look to see what she could 'read' from his face. Was he in a good or a bad mood? Her reactions were then governed by what she saw 'written' in his face. If there was a welcome on his face, all would be well. She could relax and enjoy their evening together. At other times, however, there was not a smile but a frown. Then she would be miserable for the rest of the evening, which would usually be spent in total silence. When we began to explore the meaning of this behaviour, something interesting emerged. The husband said that, quite unknown to his wife, he was playing the same game as she was! He would look at her face when she came through the door to see what kind of mood she was in, and then he would govern his reactions according to what he saw. But I was curious about who was setting up whom? At once, the wife began to think about her childhood. I asked her how she used to behave when she got home from school each day. What was she aware of as she used to go through the door of her house? The wife became sad, and recalled the fear she had of going home to the stormy and unpredictable relationship between her father and mother. She found it useful to look at their faces to 'read' the prevailing mood when she walked through the door. If there were black looks, the outcome was usually that she'd be sent to bed without tea or television. If there were smiles, then she could breathe a sigh of relief. The woman was amazed to find *she was behaving towards her husband as she had done with her mother and father*. She began to explore the possibility of entering her matrimonial home without such fear. I invited her to enter as she felt, in the here-and-now, instead of how she used to feel when she was a little girl. Without realizing it, both partners were mirroring each other's moods and producing a great deal of unnecessary unhappiness. Only as such unfinished business from our past is uncovered and let go of, can we deal with our present experiences more creatively. Counselling can be a very useful place in which to make such excavations in the presence of an accepting and understanding helper.

A further area in which unresolved issues from our past can destroy the happiness of our present life is found in many second marriages. The statistics are not encouraging. It appears that more second marriages fail than first marriages, and the latter are currently running at about one in three. I am convinced that one of the major causes of this social phenomenon is that too many people bring into their second marriages the unfinished business – the pain and the bitterness – which belong to the former marriage. The wounds from their first marriage being still unhealed, they must expend much time and energy in protecting themselves from further hurt, which in practical terms usually involves a greater distancing than their new partner finds satisfactory. The second husband or wife, therefore, is often found picking up the results of the hurt experienced by their partners in their previous marriage. Or, it can happen that the anger and humiliation felt by a wife regarding her ex-husband's treatment of her is transferred to her new husband who becomes the 'whipping boy' for what happened in the past. She couldn't trust her first husband, so she watches her new one like a hawk, checking up on his every movement and late appearance. Only as we allow the past to be the *past*, instead of an inappropriate re-hash in our present, can we move towards a new life built on love and trust. Nowhere is this radical change in our attitudes more necessary than in the important area of self-perception.

13 The inability to love myself

Talking to people as regularly as I do, it is quite apparent (to me, at any rate) that many problems which couples find hard to resolve concern the way in which they perceive themselves. They tell me of their shortcomings, how awful they really are inside, how ashamed of themselves they feel, how guilty they feel; and you don't have to be a mind-reader to hear that such people don't like themselves very much, if at all. Their role within the marriage appears to be that of the under-dog, making all the concessions and asking for nothing in return. Nature being what it is, the exploited give off very strong signals to the exploiters, and victims give off unmistakable signs to the rescuers. They frequently pair off.

One woman had this under-dog script deeply ingrained into her, and it was one of the factors which led to her subsequent depression. In the course of her therapy, she discovered a basic conflict within herself: how could she become wholly who she really was, while at the same time be who her husband wanted her to be? She knew that any growth in the direction of self-fulfilment would radically alter the way in which her marriage had hitherto been conducted. Here is the seed-bed of many potential, and actual, disagreements between couples. For most of them it is a painful experience, and very often partners will opt for pleasing the other person rather than expressing joyfully their own inner self. Given the choice, most of us will choose the way of self-sacrifice in order to enrich our partner and their happiness.

I realize the good, apparently laudable, motives which lie behind this approach to married life. After all, isn't self-sacrifice to be regarded as a virtue? Are we not rightly taught from the cradle to 'consider other people first'? And isn't self-interest regarded almost universally as a despicable and destructive trait? Here I have to lay myself on the line, and challenge the assumptions behind these three questions. Instead of a long defence of why I do so, let me instead share a story with you from my own experience which I trust will illustrate what I'm getting at.

It happened during my studies in Chicago. I can picture the scene as I write. There we were, a group of doctoral students, sitting around the coffee-stained tables of the seminary. We had spent six months working with one another and our professor, Phil Anderson, on the issue of 'Personal Transformation'. As the seminars drew to a close, we had to provide a written paper on one aspect of what we had been trying to achieve by way of our own personal growth. I knew just the thing to please Phil. I knew the kind of paper he would appreciate, and on which I could get my vital 'A' grade. But it wasn't the paper that I wanted to write. I wrestled with the question: whom should I please? Phil or myself? I decided to please myself – and risk the 'A' grade. I wrote about my struggle with anger, how I had discovered its origins deep within me, how it had manifested itself during my life, how I had tried to suppress it, avoid it, deny it. I poured out my soul in that paper and felt that, in the writing of it, I had been healed somewhere deep inside. The 'day of judgement' arrived on the last day of our course. I confessed to Phil how I had struggled with the subject, and finally told him that I had decided to write a paper which would please me, rather than him. 'But that's where you're wrong, Tony,' he said. 'Didn't you realize that writing a paper which pleased you gives me far more pleasure than writing one to please me?' Brought up on a diet of pleasing other people, and putting myself down, this was an unusual experience for me. Somebody could actually be pleased when I pleased myself! Phil's affirmation has stayed with me ever since. Of course, I do realize that I am not living in a world exactly teeming with Phil Andersons; even so, I can still take the risk of affirming myself when occasion demands.

What has this to do with the problems found in married life? I suppose in the end it has to do with how widely you define love. The 'others first', 'sacrifice yourself', 'avoid self-centredness' philosophy is clearly wrong at this point. For these injunctions, operating in so many miserable marriages today, omit one essential element: *self-love.* Here I value the words of Eric Fromm:

> The idea expressed in the Biblical 'Love thy neighbour as thyself!' implies that respect for one's own integrity and uniqueness, love for and understanding of one's own self, cannot be separated from respect and love and understanding for another individual. The love for my own self is inseparably connected with the love for any other being . . .
>
> From this it follows that my own self must be as much an object of my love as another person. *The affirmation of one's own life, happiness, growth, freedom is rooted in one's capacity to love* . . . If an individual is able to love productively, he loves himself too; if he can love *only* others, he cannot love at all.[18]

Problems frequently occur among couples, therefore, not because they love themselves too much, but too little. In fact, many of us have inherited such a bad self-image from our past that we find little to value in ourselves. Our self-perception is that of the 'ugly duckling'. The 'others first' idea merely serves to reinforce our basic sense of worthlessness. Fromm's words remind us of the appropriateness of actually learning to love ourselves. This wider definition of love is mirrored in the words of Dr Scott Peck: 'I define love thus: The will to extend one's self for the purpose of nurturing one's own or another's growth.[19]

Notice that in Scott Peck's estimation, the nurture of one's own self is regarded with as much importance as the nurture of our partner. *They are not alternatives.* The truth for me is that unless I can love my own uniqueness, and nurture my own growth, I will be unable to love the uniqueness of my partner and nurture her own growth. To repeat Fromm's words, 'The love for my own self is inseparably connected with the love for any other being.' So often in the counselling of couples, it appears that each partner is trying to love the other person *out of an empty vessel.* Having little or no self-regard, they find themselves trying to love the other person out of their emptiness instead of out of their fullness. To talk to such people about 'self-sacrifice', therefore, is tantamount to kicking someone when they're down!

The idea of loving one's self might sound as if I am trying to turn two thousand years of history on its head, for does not the Bible teach, 'Love thy neighbour'. The truth is that we have failed to appreciate the vital corollary, '. . . as thyself'. You simply can't love other people satisfactorily until you learn to love yourself; you cannot forgive others until you learn to forgive yourself; you cannot nurture another's growth until you adequately nurture your own. You can't share with your partner something you don't possess. But does not this approach smack dangerously of rampant selfishness? Listen to Erich Fromm again:

> *Selfishness and self-love, far from being identical, are actually opposites*. The selfish person does not love himself too much but too little; in fact he hates himself. This lack of fondness and care for himself . . . leaves him empty and frustrated. He is necessarily unhappy and anxiously concerned to snatch from life the satisfactions which he blocks himself from attaining. He seems to care too much for himself, but actually he only makes an unsuccessful attempt to cover up and compensate for his failure to care for his real self . . . *It is true that selfish persons are incapable of loving others, but they are not capable of loving themselves either.*[20]

The unpleasant phenomena of self-indulgence and self-absorption – far from being signs of loving one's self too much – are actually grotesque caricatures of self-love. The paradox is simply this: in order to love my partner adequately I must learn to love myself more, not less. It is out of that essential self-affirmation and self-acceptance that I shall be able to move out, sacrificially if need be, to meet the needs of those around me. If, on the other hand, my basic attitude towards myself is one of self-disgust, self-loathing and self-rejection, not only will I be totally unable to meet the need for nurture in my beloved, but at the same time *I shall be unable to accept the love which she shows towards me.*

As I write this, one particular couple comes to mind. One of the woman's characteristics was an entirely self-centred attitude towards life. She indulged her every whim. Happiness, for the wife, seemed to lie in possessing what she did not have, only to find that the new possession was soon in the cupboard, discarded and unappreciated. Nothing seemed to satisfy her. She indulged her craving for sweets and chocolates. Unless the world revolved around her and her needs, the world was a living hell, both for her and those in her family. To the outside world, it appeared that this woman was totally absorbed in loving herself. But when I checked out with her whether or not that was true, she told me with tears in her eyes, 'Of course not! I really hate myself!' The love she craves and demands cannot, in fact, be received. It runs off her like water from a duck's back. She confesses she has nothing to give to her husband and children because of this insatiable appetite for *substitute love*. In order to love herself, she must open those blocked-off places within her where her deepest pain and hurt lie, and learn to expose herself to the love of her self in order that she may be open to the love of other people. She needs to learn how to effect a radical change in her self-perception.

So, paradoxically, as I learn to love and accept myself, I am more able to love and accept others. Once I am in touch with, and rejoicing in, my own uniqueness, I can be in touch with and rejoice in your uniqueness too. From a basis of being truly 'centred' in my self, I then have the inner resources to be fully committed to your on-going growth. I do not have to guard selfishly the meagre resources within our relationship; from my own base of well-being I can give myself to you, and learn together how to increase our love, wonder and joy. It was people like Phil Anderson who taught me how to do this, and I didn't find it easy to change the please-other-people habits of a lifetime. I'm just glad that there were enough people around me who loved me enough to help me make the attempt. I couldn't be sharing this with you now unless to some extent I had succeeded.

So far as the problems in your marriage stem from a highly developed sense of your own worthlessness and self-devaluation, such impairment in your self-perception would figure highly on the counselling agenda. Rarely do people enter counselling complaining of a 'deficiency in my self-esteem'. Rather, they will come complaining of feeling depressed, a lack of motivation, physical tiredness, 'out of sorts', or say in an apologetic tone, that they are 'just a waste of space'. Chances are they have taken this catalogue to their GP first of all, but most perceptive doctors will spot the underlying cause and refer their patient to a counsellor. I can scarcely remember a client suffering from depression who did not have, as an important ingredient in his condition, a profound belief in his own worthlessness. The discovery of his own self-worth will have an equally profound effect upon his relationship to his wife and family.

For one thing, he will no longer allow his family to treat him like the proverbial doormat. Possessing an appropriate sense of his own value, he will be able to appreciate more clearly the value of others. No longer a walking apology, this man will assert his rights and accept his responsibilities within the family. He will defend his integrity and the integrity of others. Now able to accept himself as he is, he will be more ready to accept others as they are. Loving himself, he will be open to the loving affirmation of his family, and be able to express in word and deed his love for them. Aware now of the appropriateness of expressing his own needs, he becomes able to respond more fully to the needs of others in his family. Whereas in his depressed state he was a drain on the family, now he is an important resource. It really does pay to learn how to love yourself.

But some of you might object: 'Doesn't all this smack of narcissistic indulgence?' By no means. There is all the difference in the world between narcissism and self-love. The original myth of Narcissus reveals him falling love with *his own image*, not with himself. It is with self-image, not self-love that narcissists are concerned. Alexander Lowen writes: 'It is self-acceptance that is lacking in narcissistic individuals . . . Without self-acceptance, there is no self-love.[21] Narcissism is what emerges as a substitute for loving oneself. In spite of appearances to the contrary, the narcissist does not love himself; he merely seeks to inflate his ego by way of compensation. He becomes image-centred, and Lowen is right when he describes the narcissistic personality pattern as 'a denial of the true self'. True self-love and self-acceptance are at the opposite end of the spectrum from narcissism.

14
My expectations and assumptions about marriage

'Assumptions and expectations', writes Moira Fryer of RELATE, 'don't half bedevil early marriage.'[22] It might be helpful if we understand an 'assumption' as something we simply take for granted, while an 'expectation' is more a matter of actively hoping for something. These assumptions and expectations, as they are brought with us into marriage, form a very powerful desire which we expect our partner to fulfil. I will set out two areas where such expectations operate, in order to illustrate how they can affect your relationship and what happens when your expectations are not met. It is out of this basic disappointment with marriage, when your expectations are not met, that the need for marital counselling may arise.

Role expectations

During the past two decades, the fall-out from what used to be known as the Women's Liberation Movement (a misnomer, in fact, since the movement at its best had as much to do with the liberation of men as with women) has affected not only our judicial system regarding 'equal opportunities' but also the way we think about male and female roles. In life-before-Germaine-Greer, male-chauvinist-piggery prevailed. The male's role was considered more important than the female's; the 'little woman's' place was in the home. What is sometimes referred to as the 'KKK' syndrome (Kinder, Kirche, Küchen – children, church, and kitchen) played havoc with the female sense of pride and self-respect. She was regarded in some places as an appendage of her husband, and some religious cultures in the Middle East still treat women so.

British cultural expectations are now changing, however, and the old KKK programme will no longer do for the majority of women. Indeed, some women object to *men* writing about women's rights as it appears to smack of male patronization. However, there seems little doubt that stereotyped male and female roles in our society contribute significantly to problems in a marriage. A lot will depend on the gifts and aptitudes of the two people concerned but, if the individual uniqueness and value of each partner is not observed and defended by the other, serious problems can arise.

When one partner in a marriage feels disrespect for who they are, and what they do, trouble is already brewing. While her problem is about undervaluation, his problem might be that he doesn't see this as a problem at all. For instance, a woman told me of the unhappiness she felt by being ignored by her husband, especially regarding her work. She held down a very responsible job at a hospital. He seemed to have the idea that his work was more important than hers. He would never discuss her job or indeed show any interest in it. Showing no regard or respect for her work, he was in fact subtly devaluing her. She tried to make him aware of this problem but he wouldn't hear of it. Respect for her self finally led to a confrontation of her husband, and he with some reluctance, and a good deal of resentment, finally agreed to see me *about her problem*.

It is often found, of course, that attitudes such as these are inherited from the family within which we are brought up. They are frequently passed down from father to son without a great deal of thought about the matter. Equally, a woman can learn the submissive and subservient role from her mother, who learned it from her mother, and so on. The male and female roles, therefore, become stereotyped and swallowed whole with little or no awareness. The *status quo* appears untouchable.

When couples go into counselling, it is often necessary to identify and explore the marital-role expectations under which they are operating. Each partner is invited to express what expectations they hold and what part they are playing in the current marital conflict. For example, who makes the final decisions in this family? Who does most of the household chores and work around the house? Who holds the purse-strings? Who usually initiates sex?

Who exercises discipline within the family? Naturally, such questions are not fired at the couple by an inquisitorial counsellor, but there might be a need to check out with the couple how far such issues are contributing to their present unhappiness. The couple themselves will bring to counselling their own agenda, the way they see what the main problem is, and the counsellor will assist them to express how they feel about the expectations their partner has of them, and how far they are unwilling to meet these expectations. The couple will be invited to say how far they are satisfied with the way things are in their marriage, and to pinpoint areas of dissatisfaction. At the heart of many family rows lies a grievance about the role they are expected to play in the marriage, whether it is the wife as family skivvy, or the husband as the meal ticket.

Assumptions about dependency and independency

These represent opposite poles in our attitudes towards other people, and they often lurk behind many of the presenting symptoms in marriage counselling. They can prove damaging to our most intimate relationships because, in their extreme forms, they distort healthy ways of relating to one another.

Take the issue of *dependence*. This is the natural state into which every child is born. It is totally dependent upon others, especially mother, to attend to its survival needs, and without which the new-born infant would die. At this infantile stage of our human development, dependency is a totally natural state to be in. The infant cannot feed itself (though it seems to need no teaching as to what a nipple is and does!) or attend to any of its most basic needs; it is, in other words, helpless. In this condition, power and resources belong *outside* the new-born infant. Therefore, others come to be perceived as all-powerful, and that is a correct perception for an infant. In this stage of our development, dependency is an appropriate yet temporary condition. However, it is a sad fact that some people can get stuck in this condition, particularly due to later 'smothering' in which our natural desire to be independent is either thwarted or punished. Dependency then becomes a permanent state in which we live, convinced of our own innate powerlessness and weakness, and at the same time convinced of the all-sufficiency and invincibility of others.

Some family 'power games' ensure that parents keep the upper hand by enforcing upon their children an unhealthy degree of dependency. The growing child is never allowed to develop his or her potential; it is kept in an infantile condition, reinforced by reminders of the dangers of doing things for itself. Such children grow up systematically deprived of knowledge and experience of their own inner power and coping mechanisms. In order to retain parental power and control, the infant must be kept down. The dependency is fostered in order to keep intact the parents' own need to be needed by their children. A young woman told me how her mother constantly undermined her enthusiasm for her forthcoming marriage. Instead of encouragement and affirmation, this young woman received only discouragement and pessimism. 'You'll never get married,' she was told. 'He'll find someone else before then!' Behind this negativity lies the mother's need to be needed by her daughter, and the mother's fear of what would happen to her *own* marriage once there was only her and her husband at home. Here is just one example of parental claustrophobia which inhibits the natural development in a young woman towards becoming her own person. It also illustrates how our inbuilt confidence about ourselves and our choices can be seriously eroded by such parental treatment.

It is in ways such as these that we grow up with our infantile patterns of behaviour intact. Nothing was ever challenged. When we get married we bring with us the idea that 'mummy does everything' and, of course, most of us are in for a nasty shock when 'mummy' has other ideas! Children who were reared to leave everything lying around the house, waiting for mummy or daddy to pick them up, are in need of re-education within a marriage. This is just one form which 'dependency' can take in a relationship. Other forms include emotional and financial dependency and variants of the 'daddy-do-it' syndrome. A young man in his late twenties came to see me complaining of his inability to leave home and start a new life of his own. Mummy was still collecting his wages each week, and arranging his finances for him. At the age of 9, perhaps, such behaviour might have seemed quite normal; but at 29? What happens when such people, who have been damaged like this man, enter marriage? They enter marriage as a broken reed, a clinging ivy which would fall down if it were not so tightly attached to the partner's neck. Such apparent 'reliance' might appear to be a charming attribute, reinforcing the strength of the one on whom the dependent partner relies, but from a long-term point of view it is usually catastrophic. The expectation that he or she will 'look after me' needs exploring and letting go. There could, of course, be a serious condition of immaturity in such people, what in the counselling industry we call the Peter Pan Syndrome.

J. M. Barrie's famous character is, at first sight, a charming little boy. When Wendy asks why he ran away, Peter Pan replies, 'Because I heard Father and Mother talking of what I was to be when I became a man. I want always to be a little boy and have fun.' Thousands of men are like Peter Pan in their attitudes towards life. They represent this crisis of dependency in its most dramatic form, although the phenomenon is not merely a masculine one. There are many women who wish to remain little girls, and never grow up. As we noticed in the chapter on models of partnership, the kind of relationship which represents Peter Pan and Wendy (you-mummy/me-little-boy) has its counterpart in you-daddy/me-little-girl. While such relationships might have an initial attraction, it is almost inevitable that sooner or later one of the partners will get fed up playing such games, and then the fat is in the matrimonial fire. It is at this point that counselling could help sort out the scripts on which the relationship has formerly been based, and to see how far creative changes might be made to the satisfaction of both partners. While one partner is going to have to grow up, the other is going to have to let them have their independence.

The issues of *independence* lie at the other end, and introduce us to the attitude which says, 'I can do it on my own without any help from you.' The opposite of letting others do everything for you is allowing others to do nothing for you. Here is the self-made person, the all-sufficient character, who expects and accepts no help from anyone. They become self-reliant to the point of excluding the other person altogether. Maybe they have a personal history of other people letting them down badly when they were in a childhood state of dependence, and they learned to distrust their world and their environment. Never again would they allow themselves to be in a situation where they had to depend on the goodwill of other people. Past hurts and disappointments are brought with them into the present, affecting other people who had nothing to do with the original painful experiences. Bringing this kind of attitude into a marriage poses serious problems, especially for the partner who wishes to get close enough to give and receive intimacy.

In their attempt to remain invulnerable, the independent personality must shut out the other person, sometimes completely. They may never be able to allow others to get close to them, emotionally, although most of them will function sexually in a perfunctory sort of way. In sex, they will tend to be the technicians rather than the artists of love. It's just that there will be no true 'letting go' with the other person, no opening up to them about who they truly are, and above all, no loss of control. They are often so badly affected by past pain and disappointment that they become incapable of close and intimate relationships. This kind of defensive barrier, carved out of the terror and anxiety of early childhood, is brought into the counselling room, not by the independent character (who will never admit to a problem anyway), but by the distraught partner who 'cannot get through' to the person they love. Their partner can resemble the embattled character so brilliantly described in the words of Paul Simon:

I have my books
And my poetry to protect me;
I am shielded in my armour,
Hiding in my room,
Safe within my womb,
I touch no one and no one touches me.

I am a rock,
I am an island:
And a rock feels no pain,
And an island never cries.[23]

Clearly, those who are married to partners with this outlook on life are in for severe disappointment of their expectations for a close, warm and intimate relationship.

As I was writing these words, a woman arrived for an appointment. The timing was quite uncanny, since she started to unfold a problem she was having within her own marriage concerning this issue of chronic independence. She felt her husband was 'shutting her out'; that he felt he must 'cope on his own'; how he rejected her help, and whenever she tried to get close to him, physically, she was pushed away. 'I can't stand being touched,' he told her. His inner emotional pain had been projected on to his body. The words of Paul Simon are both poignant and accurate in their description of this husband. Many people 'can't get through' to their partners, and they resemble the painful image painted so memorably in 'I am a rock'. This 'island' image is also referred to by the late Dr Paul Tournier when he wrote:

> I remember a woman who had come to speak to me of her very serious worries. At the end of our interview I asked her, 'What does your husband think of all that?' 'Oh', she blurted out, 'my husband is a mysterious island. I am forever circling around it but never finding a beach where I may land.' I understand her, for it is true. There are men who are like mysterious islands. They protect themselves against any approach.[24]

With due deference to Dr Tournier, it is my experience that such 'mysterious islands' are by no means the exclusive haven of men! There are many occasions when I hear from husbands that it is their wives who represent this independent, 'island' characteristic.

Counsellors are well acquainted with this dependency/independency axis; we usually refer to it as the 'compulsively attached/compulsively detached' personality pattern. Serious psychopathic elements can lie underneath this pattern of relating to others. It is strange how often these two different personality patterns meet and fall in love with each other – almost against all reason. It is not difficult, therefore, to see that in such marriages there are two conflicting sets of expectations operating and there can be no satisfying both at the same time. Counselling could help to explore these situations sympathetically to both partners, perhaps by taking a look at the concept of *interdependence*.

15
Thinking single

A further recurring problem people bring to counselling concerns the failure to make the adaptation, both in thought and in action, to the married state. One wife said, 'He seems to want all the privileges of being married, while avoiding any kind of responsibility.' This husband was, in fact, behaving as if he were single within his marriage. His previous life-style remained intact. Carla Lane, in her own inimitable style, has created a classic stereotype of this kind of man in the character Billy in *Bread* (BBC1). He is married to Julie, but he has never yet really left his home across the road. 'Thinking single' is that attitude that fails to take account of the commitment to the *partnership* of marriage, and the courage to work at it.

Initially, there will be some growing pains as both partners come to terms with leaving their singleness behind. No one would expect all these profound changes to be made overnight, merely by the possession of a marriage certificate. After many years of preparing young people for marriage, I came to the conclusion that this element of the loss of singleness needed early and careful attention. I began to recognize that *getting married involves one of the most profound developmental losses in life.* I knew this from the way in which some young marrieds seemed to bring with them a real, yet unfocused, sense of sadness into what everyone expected to become one of the most joyful experiences we can have. There appeared on many occasions to be a kind of sad shadow hanging over one or other of the partners, which could find expression either in general moodiness or often in tears. 'I know I'm silly,' she would say, 'and I know I ought to be happy, but I just feel very sad about something.' The 'something' often turns out to be the natural, yet hidden, grief over the loss of singleness.

I remember the first time I risked beginning my pre-marital counselling with a young couple by asking them what they were going to *miss* most about being married. Here they were, starry-eyed and so much in love, with wedding bells in their ears, hardly at first able to comprehend my question. Their eyes, quite naturally, were on the *future;* I wanted first of all to turn their eyes to the *past* they were leaving behind for good. Eventually, in order to satisfy my curiosity, they began to talk about leaving home. 'What will you miss most?' I asked her. She sat and thought carefully before replying. 'Well, there's my room, I suppose,' she said. There was another long silence, after which I asked her if she could say goodbye to it? She began to soliloquize on her room, describing it in minute detail, and then – suddenly – she burst into tears. 'Everything's going to change, isn't it?' she inquired between sobs. 'Yes,' I said, 'and you need to appreciate that, and weep about it for a while.' This was not a case of me upsetting someone unnecessarily. That grief of hers was within her *already*, though unrecognized, and she was about to drag it into her marriage, thereby contaminating it from the start with the shadow of sadness. This train of thought led her fiancé to think about what he would be leaving behind, and we had a most constructive evening together getting the submerged grief out of the way, so that this would not spoil the happiness of their forthcoming marriage.

Thinking single in marriage also often concerns attitudes towards parents and in-laws. Where do they now fit in with the new pattern of their child's marriage? There are many parents who are marvellous at letting their children go, and in spite of their curiosity to know how things are, they keep their curiosity in check until their son or daughter wants to tell them. Others, however, resemble the proverbial 'out-laws' rather than in-laws, interfering at every turn. They make decisions for their newly-married child and criticize their choice of partner, with the implied message that – of course – they would have been better off staying at home. Meanwhile, the son or daughter tries to keep up the balancing act between pleasing their parents and pleasing their partner. Many fail in this gallant attempt of walking the matrimonial tightrope. Meeting the expectations of intrusive parents and those of one's partner is more than most of us can manage. The priority of the commitment to the marriage is vital, and part of the loss of singleness entails saying goodbye to our parents in terms of our childhood relationship to them. We still love them, but there is now a prior claim to our love. It is hard to say (and do) this, but it is precisely at this point that we can understand what thinking single in a marriage is: it is *the avoidance of the losses we experience in losing our singleness*, hence the temptation to prolong it, inappropriately, within our marriage. The implications of this unwillingness to make these painful adjustments when we get married are potentially damaging to many relationships today.

There are, of course, many other implications for our marriages when we forget that we are now a partnership, and behave as if we were single. Former relationships would loom large in this consideration, and how far it is helpful to retain them. There are attitudes which need to be adopted in order for us to think of ourselves as a 'couple' rather than as single people. I well remember the first day of my own honeymoon in Paris, walking around that beautiful city leading my wife with one hand, and with my *Michelin Guide* in the other. That evening Jan exploded, naturally though unexpectedly, at my unthinking behaviour. For years she had been a competent nursing sister and later a deaconess, holding responsible positions, and here she was being led around Paris like a child. My consciousness was raised about thirty feet by that episode, and the next day it was me who was being shown around Paris. It simply had not occurred to me that Jan could read a map as well as I could, if not better! My thinking single was operating here, and I was unaware of infantilizing my wife. We laughed about it later, as we opened a bottle of wine together, but it was one of those experiences which made me check out my own assumptions and to appreciate more fully what being a partnership actually meant. I needed consciously to raise my estimation of Jan's capabilities, as I have had need to do on more than one occasion since.

Another of my own learning experiences brings me to the subject of finances within a marriage. Matters of finance and the handling of the couple's income(s) present a familiar problem area to many people. When Jan and I were discussing this issue, my mind was fixed on the *amount* of housekeeping money she should have, rather than the *appropriateness* of housekeeping money in an open relationship. Before some of my female readers choke on such a suggestion, I must confess that this is just how I was brought up to think (role expectations again!); heaven knows, money was a constant cause of uproar and division in my family. The thought never crossed my mind that 'housekeeping' was intended for 'housekeepers', not for an equal partner. The obvious answer (for us at least) was a joint bank account so no one was giving anyone money; for us it works superbly, in spite of my early – and groundless – fears of imminent bankruptcy.

Couples need to be as open and honest about money matters as they are in other aspects of their relationship, but some find this hard to do. Money is an area where trust and understanding are not always exercised, and there is often jealousy and suspicion bred through the wage packet. Of course, knowing how human nature works, other problems can lurk craftily behind money matters ('I'm not getting enough' could be applied to other areas of the relationship) while using 'money' as the shield. The wise counsellor knows this and can carefully invite the couple to discover other areas where they are not satisfied with what they are getting – time, perhaps?

It is very easy to 'think single' when deciding how to share the family income. 'His' and 'hers' might look cute on the bathroom towels, but where money is concerned there needs to be some provision for 'ours'. A couple I knew had separated because of financial disagreements. The story was a familiar one. The careful and competent management of the family income by the wife was being sabotaged by the husband's overspending; he exhibited a chronic inability to deny himself anything he wanted. In keeping with the time-honoured maxim, 'An ounce of experience is worth a pound of advice,' he had to come to terms with managing his own flat after they separated. He was surprised to find that he just could not keep us his boozing bouts with his mates *and* pay the rent. The couple are now back together again trying to find a new and workable way round the handling of their income as a partnership.

Thinking single, therefore, is a constant source of friction within marriages. But it is vital to notice that the opposite of thinking single is not the 'Siamese twin' syndrome. We are not meant to be glued to one another, nor denied an individuality all of our own. We are not intended to be clones of our spouses, nor slaves either. Given that the first commitment is to the *partnership* (and backing one another up when the families try to interfere in this), there can be plenty of space left to develop as an individual. It is the neglect of one's individuality, submerging oneself and one's separate identity into an amorphous 'coupledom' that gives rise to problems later on in a marriage. It is a welcome sign in our culture that we (and especially women) are now able to explore and express ourselves and our gifts as unique individuals while being married at the same time. In spite of what men have been telling women for years, bringing up children and looking after the home do not always fulfil a wife's potential. For some, maybe; but not for all.

The beautiful poem of Kahlil Gibran gives, for me, the right balance of interdependence in a close and intimate relationship:

> Love one another, but make not a bond of love:
> Let it rather be a moving sea between the shores of your souls . . .
> Sing and dance together and be joyous, but let each one of you be alone . . .
> And stand together yet not too near together:
> For the pillars of the temple stand apart,
> And the oak tree and the cypress grow not in each other's shadow.[25]

16 Sexual fidelity

If Dr Peck is correct in his assumption that 'falling in love' is chiefly motivated by erotic and sexual desires, then most couples will enter into their relationship with some expectations of sexual fulfilment and enjoyment. High on the list of any survey into modern marriage will come the disappointment that many couples express concerning the failure of such expectations.

In the past three decades there has been a major revolution in sexual attitudes and, for good or ill, we can safely say that sex is out of the Victorian cupboard. Women appear to have gained most through the 'liberation' movement, and the reasons for this are not hard to find. For centuries, female sexuality had been kept in the shadows of men's needs; indeed, sexual enjoyment had become almost exclusively a male expectation and privilege. That women had a natural right to share in such expectations came as a profound shock to large sections of the Western (male) world. The old adage of 'lying back and thinking of England' had too much truth in it to remain a laughing matter. Women became increasingly concerned for their personal sexual liberation, and the repercussions of this proper concern are still being felt in many relationships today.

If a relationship had been based on the expectation that sexual pleasure was the sole right of the male partner, and the role of the woman was merely to act as a passive vehicle of her husband's pleasure, there was bound to be a crisis when the sexual revolution invaded that union. The sexual liberation of women profoundly threatened the male population as their wives began to assert themselves. Poor sexual performance, unimaginative and repetitive styles of making love, sheer indifference to their partner's needs together with a marked lack of affection and gentleness, were exposed as women dared to confront male chauvinism. It was not surprising, therefore, that the 'Women's Lib' movement came under strong attack from men, who, sensing they now had *their* backs to the wall, fought back with whatever weapons they could muster, including mockery, ridicule and a forced sense of humour.

The distinction between expectation and performance found artistic expression in the outstanding film *Ryan's Daughter*, directed by Robert Bolt. The heroine (played by Sarah Miles) experiences the difference between her husband's wedding-night approach of 'Wham! Bam! Thank you, ma'am!', which left her both mystified and unfulfilled, and that of the army officer who affirms her femininity and sexuality and in a caring way helped her to become sexually awakened to her deepest sensual nature. This was not, as mistakenly thought, a case of a man 'giving her an orgasm'; rather, in their tender act of love each found their true selves expressed in sexual terms, the themes of harmony and oneness being portrayed in some brilliant (and Oscar winning) photography.

Many of the issues and insights of the 'women's movement' are now part and parcel of our culture. One writer is of the opinion that, 'From the vantage-point of the twenty-first century, we will regard the "women's movement" as the most significant and consequential social phenomenon of the present era'.[26] Hence, couples arrive in counselling today against the background of this revolution which has just as much to do with the spiritual and social emancipation of women as it does with their sexual freedom. One factor, however, constantly arises, and that focuses on the important issue of *sexual exclusiveness*. In various forms, this issue lies at the heart of much heated debate.

There are, of course, some very strong traditional, cultural and religious reasons for the expectation of sexual exclusiveness within a relationship. While we may be in what sociologists call a 'post-Christian age', it is nevertheless true that the laws of our country have been greatly influenced by traditional Christian morality. There are the biblical warrants against adultery and the strong emphasis on chastity before marriage and faithfulness within it. Such an emphasis on exclusivity is enshrined in the familiar marriage vows, '. . . and forsaking all others, be faithful to him/her as long as you both shall live . . .' A similar vow is included in civil weddings at local Registry Offices. We have come to expect, therefore, through history and tradition, that our partners will remain 'faithful'.

This traditional view was overturned during the sexual revolution of the 1960s, and no matter how much some people may wring their hands and lament the 'immorality' and 'permissiveness' of our age, attitudes towards sexual activity have undergone a major moral reversal. Today, people are much more likely to abstain from sex outside their marriage for fear of contracting AIDS than for any religious or moral considerations. The sexual revolution had many practical results, not least the critical review of the traditional Christian 'package deal' on sex. As this was exposed to a searching examination, some pretty unhealthy attitudes were found crawling around inside. For instance, one writer said:

> Much of the sexual ethic of western Christendom . . . regarded matter as degraded, nature as the creation of a demonic god, women as inferiors, and sex as lust to be repressed or expressed only within marriage. Had Augustine not felt so guilty for his mistress, the Middle Ages might have recognized that sexual feelings were one of the delightful gifts of the Creator. As it was, Christianity fell into an anti-erotic posture: glorifying virginity, degrading woman, linking sex to guilt, discouraging romance, denying the flesh, casting suspicion upon sensuality.[27]

(Should anyone doubt the validity of Sam Keen's assessment, I would invite them to compare the way in which his statement is fully vindicated by the hysterical reaction by some Christians to the Martin Scorsese film, 'The Last Temptation of Christ', first screened in this country in 1988.)

In 1978, Dr James Nelson, Professor of Christian Ethics at United Theological Seminary at Minneapolis-St Paul, wrote an important book called *Embodiment*, which exposed the shortcomings of the previously accepted view of morality. He examined the case both for and against sexual exclusivity:

> The nuclear family model has carried with it an image of marriage as an encapsulated sphere, hermetically sealed from relationships of emotional depth with those outside it. But it is both unrealistic and unfair to expect that one person can always meet the partner's companionate needs . . . If the gospel truly invites us to the greatest possible realization of human capacity in interdependence with others, then marriage ought to be open to precisely that.[28]

Dr Nelson makes an important point in the arguments for and against sexual exclusiveness, namely the need for permanence in marital relationships: 'Given current pressures on marriages, it is argued that the choice for many couples might well be between sexual exclusivity and marital permanence – and the latter is the greater value.'[29]

Another Christian writer, Dr Jack Dominian, reinforces this argument for permanence: 'The real evil of our age is not the permissiveness of sexual pleasure but the impermanency of relationships whereby, through transience and divorce, human beings become stepping stones of temporary exploitation . . .'[30]

Frankly, most of us want both sexual exclusivity *and* marital permanence within our own marriages, and of course there are many relationships where this expectation is met. I believe that there is an urgent need, however, to broaden the concept of 'faithfulness' from its previous application solely to sex. There are many marriages where it is possible for one partner to 'obey all the rules' of a marriage legally, yet in a totally unfeeling way, and because they never stray into other relationships be thought of as 'guiltless', or the innocent party. There are also other marriages where one partner, often in sheer desperation, has an affair and so is pronounced 'guilty'. It is the difference between the 'spirit' and the 'letter' of the law. In my opinion and experience, there are as many guilty parties who keep to the rules, as there are guilty parties who break them. However, once we broaden the concept of fidelity to include the whole quality of the relationship, a different picture emerges. Infidelity then is no longer equated with 'sex outside marriage', since the matrimonial commitment is always broader than the merely sexual. For Dr James Nelson, fidelity is:

> a commitment of emotional and physical intimacy with the partner; it means caring for the growth and fulfilment of each as a person; it is commitment to the growth of the marital relationship itself; it requires honesty, openness, and trust; it involves willingness to explore ways of opening the self to the partner at the deepest possible level, risking the pains that may come; it includes openness to secondary relationships of emotional intimacy and potential genital expression, but with commitment to the primacy of the marriage.[31]

It frequently occurs that couples come into counselling following the confession, or discovery, of 'an affair'. The relationship clearly faces a crisis. Marital expectations have been sadly let down. The following story illustrates one person's discovery in such a situation as this, and it is with his full permission that I quote it at length.

Marcus recounted the first time in his twenty-year-old marriage that he slept with another woman. The experience for him was to have far-reaching repercussions. He met a totally accepting woman to whom he felt an immediate attraction, a feeling which was reciprocated. There was an explicit invitation to him to make love to her. Marcus had never known that experience. With his wife it was a case of knocking on the door and asking permission. Whenever he made a sexual advance to his wife, a tired, sardonic, smirk would confront him – 'And what do you think you're doing?' But now he found himself wanting to respond to this other woman's invitation. His whole body, shrivelled up by the lack of warmth in his marriage, cried out for satisfaction. Marcus made love – but was also made love *to*, an entirely new experience. She rejoiced in his body, especially his genitals which his wife always dismissed with her withering, 'Do cover yourself up – you're no oil painting!' For the first time in his life, Marcus experienced a total orgasm and an emotional and physical affirmation which had been totally lacking throughout his marriage. He was engulfed by an ecstasy and a joy, such as he had previously only read about, or experienced in hearing the music of Bach and Mahler. Indeed, he said that at the height of his orgasm the music from Bach's B Minor Mass was ringing in the whole of his body, 'Sanctus, sanctus, sanctus' ('Holy, holy, holy'). As a practising Christian, his understanding of holiness was transformed into wholeness, something bodily as well as spiritual. The only shadow cast was that of immediate guilt. His partner, aware of his change of mood, asked what he was feeling. He felt guilty, he said, because he had been unfaithful to his wife. 'Yes, that's true', said the woman, 'but isn't it equally true that your wife has been unfaithful to you for the past twenty years?' Marcus knew a moment of rare insight; in that instant he recognized that what the woman had said was neither rhetoric nor an excuse for what had taken place between them. He began to reinterpret his marital experience and knew that his wife could not escape some culpability for the state of affairs which had produced such emptiness and yearning within him. Unfortunately for him, his act of 'adultery' was somewhat more concrete than the sins of omission on the part of his wife. The question arose, Who broke the marital contract first? Whose was the prior infidelity? Marcus might have been unfaithful for a night; had his wife been unfaithful to him for twenty years? Yet, society would see him as the 'guilty party'.

Harry Williams once wrote about a man in a similar situation to that of Marcus: 'He goes away a deeper, fuller person than he came in. What is seen in this is an act of charity which proclaims the glory of God'.[32] In counselling, the proper expectations of Marcus of a happy sexual relationship with his wife would be regarded with as much importance as the expectation of his wife for sexual fidelity. Also, the counsellor would invite the couple into a broader examination of their marriage in order to raise their awareness of the importance of faithfulness in areas other than the sexual.

Faithfulness, therefore, has as much to do with *acts* as *attitudes* within the field of personal relationships, and in marital counselling the awareness of this broader context often yields a greater degree of understanding by both partners.

17
Life's crises and turning points

A further and familiar batch of problems arise simply out of the normal course of life. One writer helpfully refers to these periods as the 'predictable crises of adult life'. Whenever I meet a new couple in counselling, one of the questions I have in the back of my mind is, 'Why now?' What brings this couple into counselling at this precise moment in their individual and corporate development? In other words, what is changing in their experience of life?

Psychologists inform us about certain periods of development (e.g. adolescence, mid-life transitions) when profound natural changes are taking place within us. These changes, of course, occur in each of us as part of the human process. It is often during such periods that problems arise within the marriage relationship, and although we cannot have control over the life changes themselves, we can do something about our *reactions* to such changes. It is these reactions that often constitute the problems in relationships which require exploration and resolution.

As we get older, we look back sometimes with amusement at our own naivety concerning the views we held in our younger days. There can be quite a bit of embarrassment too. Perhaps we had a rosy view of marriage, or of our partner, or imagined we had ample resources to deal with our lover's quirks and foibles. Indeed, such characteristics might have been part of their appeal. But as we grow into the relationship perhaps our levels of tolerance change and decrease, or our standards increase, our expectations might rise, and the once attractive quirk is now an unattractive menace which is driving us crazy.

There is also the issue of changing appetites and choices. Over advancing years even our staying power changes – as that wickedly accurate song, 'The Oldest Swinger in Town' reminds us: 'When it takes all night to do what you used to do all night, you're the oldest swinger in town!' The spirit might be willing, but the flesh is weak. Fashion, too, plays a large part in the choices we make. How many of us look in our wardrobes and nearly die laughing at some of the things we find there? Something similar is true of other fashions besides clothing. For instance, the changing cultural habits that have taken place during the past thirty years – the fast-food market, the take-aways down the road, modern gadgets like the micro-wave oven, holidays abroad – plus the mass media, especially TV, all these have had a profound effect upon us and our attitudes. We have higher and higher standards and expectations. The young marrieds of today expect to have a house to move into, after the white wedding and all the trimmings including the honeymoon abroad. For their parents, this all smacks of luxury beyond their wildest dreams when they got wed back in the sixties. The world is changing, and we change with it.

Nowhere is this more true than in our choice of partners. Take, for example, the young man who left home and got married, but for whom the leaving home bit was by far the more important. Marriage, for him, was an escape from an intolerable situation at home, and his motivation was less for the woman of his choice, and more for getting away from mother and father. The woman was merely the way out. For a while, his safe haven was perfect: no more nagging, no more checking up on what time he got home at night, no more fights about treating his sister fairly. Then one day, he looked again at the woman he had married. 'What on earth was I doing to choose her?' Such thoughts began to pass through his mind regularly. His headlong rush into committing holy matrimony was an *escape from* his home, rather than a *commitment to* his new wife. Paying more attention to what he was getting out of rather than getting into, he did not stop to consider the long-term consequences of his choices. He made the familiar mistake of choosing a life partner in the middle of a transitional crisis. This is nearly always fatal. Meanwhile, his wife will probably turn to marriage counselling in a desperate bid to keep the man she loves. The man's behaviour might sound callous and harsh, and so it is. But it illustrates how problems can arise in a relationship like marriage which were, in a sense, built into it and thus were ultimately inescapable; it was merely a matter of time before it erupted, for they were sitting on an emotional time-bomb.

Or, take the girl who falls in love with this boy with his baby face and winning ways. He needs mothering, she thinks; he agrees. This is fun! They marry, more parent and child than husband and wife. They are playing at houses. For a while she enjoys playing mother to her little boy; he naturally enjoys being mothered, especially if his real mothering was less than satisfactory. It's all a bit like fairyland where they live happily ever after – only of course it isn't, and they don't. After a while, as in most children's games, 'mummy' gets tired of her 'little boy'. 'He's such a wimp,' she tells her mother. 'He just lolls around the place, never lifts a finger to help, expects me to do all the work (just as she had trained him!). Suddenly, therefore, 'mūmmy' turns on him, accusing him of laziness, and tells him pretty firmly it's time to get his act together – or else. Stunned, he asks what has happened. If she is truthful, she will probably say, 'I'm bored with you.' Nature being what it is, either just before this occurs or immediately afterwards, she will almost certainly meet a strong man at the office, who is ready to sweep her off her feet into the sunset . . . It is the husband this time who will probably turn for help to save his marriage, accusing his wife of being flighty, and certainly not the woman he married.

What has happened? Her preferences have changed regarding the kind of person she wants to spend the rest of her life with – not because she's awkward, but perhaps she has now matured and may have recognized that her needs have now changed. Her natural development, and her need now to have a partner rather than a little boy around the house, provokes a crisis in the marriage. Wendy decides to leave Never-Never-Land, and Peter Pan, and make her own way in the world. The problem arose out of a developmental change in her, and somewhere in the process she must have grown enough to want to abandon her mothering role. While this seems to threaten the marriage, it really threatens only the basis on which the old contract was made. If they were both to seek joint marital counselling, this old and now obsolete script of 'Me-mummy/you-little-boy' would be quickly exposed, and an alternative might be explored on which they both could agree to start work. This would mean massive changes in the way they relate to each other, and indeed to the way in which they view their role within that marriage, but it would be at least possible to save this union.

The moral appears to be: what suits both partners at the beginning of their marriage, may not suit them both for ever. Now there are many couples who recognize this, and who are able to make constant adjustments to the relationship as they get older. They may not even realize that they are doing anything truly significant. They 'sense' what needs changing and they do it quite naturally without any form of crisis. However, many couples do not have this natural ability to adapt, to make what I call 'course corrections' on the marital journey. Marriages, therefore, need a regular update to make sure they are running on contemporary needs, not historical ones. What I needed last year from my partner might not be what I need this year. This does not imply that I am hopelessly fickle and can't make up my mind; it means I am a living, developing, changing individual whose choices will naturally have to change in accordance with my changing needs. As with other periods of natural development, *the point of change is often the point of crisis*.

The mid-life crisis is perhaps the most recognized of all our adult developmental crises. It is certainly one in which major changes can occur in the life of any couple. For males, who appear to be more affected by this phenomenon (possibly because most of the major sociological studies have been on males), it usually occurs around the late thirties and into the mid-forties. The 'Big 4–0' is an unavoidable point of transition in a man's life. One writer, who has contributed a major study of the patterns of male adult development, writes:

> The Mid-life Transition, which lasts from roughly age 40 to 45, provides a bridge from early to middle adulthood. It brings a new set of developmental tasks. The life structure again comes into question. It becomes important to ask: 'What have I done with my life? What do I really get from and give to my wife, children, friends, work, community – and self? What is it I truly want for myself and others?' A man yearns

> for a life in which his actual desires, values, talents and aspirations can be expressed.
>
> ... for the great majority of men this is a period of great struggle within the self and with the external world. Their Mid-life Transition is a time of moderate or severe crisis. They question nearly every aspect of their lives and feel that they cannot go on as before. They will need several years to form a new path or to modify the old one.[33]

So, like all other major points of transition in our lives, the 'mid-life transition' is both *natural and neutral.* It contains as much hope and possibility as it does danger and threat. It is a time for coming to terms with change, and ageing, and for daring to look into the future and catch a glimpse of the possibilities for growth and enrichment of one's life. In the familiar Levinson study, for 80 per cent of his sample of forty men, this period evoked 'tumultuous struggles within the self and with the external world'. His own words are worth noting:

> In the Mid-life Transition these neglected parts of the self urgently seek expression. A man experiences them as 'other voices in other rooms' (in Truman Capote's evocative phrase). Internal voices that have been muted for years now clamour to be heard. At times they are heard as a vague whispering, the content unclear, but the tone indicating grief over lost opportunities, outrage over betrayal by others, or guilt over betrayal by oneself. At other times they come through as a thunderous roar ... A man hears the voice of an identity prematurely rejected; of a love lost or not pursued; of a valued interest or relationship given up in acquiescence to parental or other authority; of an internal figure who wants to be an athlete or nomad or artist, to marry for love or remain a bachelor, to get rich or enter the clergy or live a sensual carefree life – possibilities set aside earlier to become what he now is. During the Mid-life Transition he must learn to listen more attentively to these voices and decide consciously what part he will give them in his life.[34]

Dr Levinson certainly captures for me what I recognized in my own 'mid-life transition'. I wept when I first read his words, thankful to find that what I had been feeling deep within me was quite normal, even predictable.

I realize, of course, that one of the limitations of Dr Levinson's studies is that it was carried out exclusively on selected *men*. A more inclusive in-depth study of life's predictable crises in the lives of both men and women can be found in the writings of Gail Sheehy, most notably in her *Passages*[35] and her later *Pathfinders*.[36] The latter work, for instance, is based on research with sixty thousand people who completed her extensive life history questionnaire, and it will repay study if you are interested to read further into this important subject.

What such studies tell us is that on our matrimonial journey we shall meet with crisis and change, and these events contain within them as much possibility of improving the quality of our relationship, in breaking out of tired and outworn attitudes and life-styles, into new ways of relating, as they do in terms of threatening the present basis of the marriage. The occasional jolt to a stale marriage can focus the mind wonderfully.

In life's crises and turning points, therefore, we find much raw material for evoking fear and apprehension, and in the objective atmosphere of the counselling room these may be both expressed and more fully understood.

Summary to Part 3

Marital problems come in all shapes and sizes, and it is true that one person's mountain might be another's mole-hill. We all have a distinctive view of life which includes our own awareness of what constitutes happiness within our marriage.

My own awareness, gained from counselling couples over many years, is that people tend to come to counselling only as a last resort. I cannot remember any couple who had not already tried patience, understanding, pleading, before they resorted to counselling. Some people come when all other avenues have failed them. At one level, this kind of behaviour is praiseworthy. No one wants to cultivate a chronic sense of inadequacy in anyone else by recommending counselling at the first matrimonial twinge. At the same time, however, it will be welcome news to many people reading this that their problems are not only shared by thousands of other people, but that there are professional services available to them whereby they can seek a remedy.

I am aware that, as you read this, maybe in the middle of a crisis in your own most intimate relationship, I have not mentioned the problem you are now struggling with. What I have tried to do is to suggest some of the root causes of eventual marriage difficulties rather than get into a woeful catalogue of everything that can go wrong with a marriage. The good news is that, when these root causes are revealed and explored, there is always hope of growth towards a new quality of happiness within the relationship, even though in the short-term it will almost certainly mean rocking the matrimonial boat. When the unhappiness is the result of avoiding painful recognition of our own shortcomings, improvement may mean facing up to, and remedying, them.

This is where many of our depressive symptoms arise. Depression is a kind of substitute suffering; it's what we feel instead of feeling something else. If I'm feeling angry and avoid its appropriate expression, the chances are that I will end up feeling depressed instead of feeling angry. I have shown where many of these real feelings might come from: those parts of myself I can't cope with; something in the past I have not yet uncovered and resolved; a chronic inability to really love myself and accept myself as intrinsically good; my expectations from marriage which were either accurate yet unfulfilled, or else unrealistic to start with; a failure to make the necessary changes from thinking single to partnership; the important area of sexual intimacy; and life's own crises. Whatever problem it is that you are thinking of bringing to counselling, be assured that it will be dealt with sympathetically; no counsellor is going to think you a fool for feeling the way you do. Counsellors are trained in the total acceptance of the other person and in the exercise of empathy towards you and your partner.

You may be surprised to find that I have not mentioned, among the problems people bring to counselling, the important matter of *communication* – or, as is often the case, the failure or breakdown in communication. One of the important functions of marriage counselling is to facilitate a better way for couples to communicate with each other, and I have devoted a whole book to this important subject. For those of you who would like to read some self-help guidelines, I recommend my earlier book, *Couples Arguing*, as a useful starting point.

PART 4: WHAT HAPPENS AT A COUNSELLING SESSION?

*Why must I suffer for not being perfect
when I can be good enough?*

18
The visit by Mr and Mrs Brown

For those of you to whom counselling may previously have appeared a mysterious pursuit, and have never been part of its process, it is essential that in this 'consumer's guide' you should be given an illustration of what goes on at a counselling session.

In this final section, let us consider how a typical marriage counselling session might sound. In the following dialogue, I will try to apply the counselling principles and process outlined earlier, in order to 'earth' it in an ordinary situation. Naturally, this dialogue has inbuilt limitations. For instance, the counsellor's approach is but one of many that could be taken, depending on the training and preferences of the counsellor concerned. Also, the problems brought by Mr and Mrs Brown may not represent the issues you are facing in your own marriage. With those considerations in mind, however, the following dialogue will provide some idea of how things might proceed.

The counsellor . . .

Catherine Henson has been counselling now for about seven years. She is part of a team of counsellors at a local counselling centre near where she lives. Although the centre operates a sliding scale of fees, none of the counsellors in this centre are actually paid, but they do have an allowance for their expenses. Catherine is married with two children, aged 10 and 8. She works two nights a week at the centre, and came into counselling by way of her own personal crisis when her mother died ten years ago. The help she found then led her to further her interest in counselling, and she subsequently attended some counsellor-training courses at the local University Adult Education department.

The story so far . . .

Arthur and Barbara Brown have been married for ten years. They have no children. Barbara teaches at a local primary school where she has been for the past four years. She is now 32, the younger of two sisters. Her mother and father died a year ago in a car accident. Arthur, now 35, is the youngest of five boys. He works in the planning department of the local City Council, and sings in the church choir. They have a comfortable home, and their joint income is more than adequate for their moderate life-style. There seem to be no financial worries. However, just recently things seemed to have changed in their relationship. Arthur has experienced Barbara as being uncharacteristically moody and somewhat distant towards him, while she has found him to be irritable and unsympathetic towards her. Long silences have taken place and a lot of their former sharing seems to have disappeared. Their sex life has diminished with their loss of feeling close to one another. Arthur is convinced it is she who has changed, and one evening he comes home to find her in floods of tears. This precipitates a crisis and in desperation Arthur suggests they find some help from somewhere. Eventually, they fix an appointment to see someone at the local counselling centre, and thus they arrive for their first appointment.

COUNSELLOR: Hello, I'm Catherine Henson. I'll be your counsellor while you're here; most people call me Cathy. You're Mr and Mrs Brown, aren't you? We're quite informal here, so is it OK if I call you Arthur and Barbara?

ARTHUR: That's fine by us, isn't it dear?

CATHY: Please sit down and make yourselves comfortable. (*In the room are three easy chairs, arranged in the form of a triangle. They sit down, a little nervously.*)

CATHY: I have all your details which you gave when you fixed the appointment, so perhaps we might begin by each of you telling me why you're here?

ARTHUR: It's the wife, you see.

CATHY: The wife?

ARTHUR: Yes, she's not right. She hasn't been for some time.

CATHY: Is that how you see it, Barbara?

BARBARA: Well, not really. I know I've not been feeling right, but he's been so intolerant and unapproachable – that hasn't helped.

CATHY: Before we continue may I just say something? It would be more helpful if instead of talking *about* one another you talked *to* one another. So instead of using 'he' or 'she', could you say 'you'? This way, you would be addressing each other, not just me. Is that OK?

BARBARA: Well, (*turning to Arthur*) you have been so intolerant to me lately.

ARTHUR: That's unfair! I've tried all ways to get her -

CATHY: Could you say 'you' instead of 'her'?

ARTHUR: . . . to get you to tell me what the trouble is, but you just sit there in a huff. I can't get through to her . . . sorry, to you. I've tried hard enough.

CATHY: Arthur is saying that the reason you're here is because you haven't been right for some time, and he can't get through to you. Have you been aware of how he's been feeling?

BARBARA: I feel I'm being blamed – that it's all my fault!

CATHY: Barbara, I hear you feel blamed for your relationship going wrong, but we're not here to establish blame or where the fault lies. We're here to try to find out what exactly is going wrong in your relationship and how you can both put it right.

ARTHUR: You see what I mean? She's not hearing you.

CATHY: Can you direct your words to your wife?

ARTHUR: Are you listening to what Cathy is saying to you?

BARBARA: Yes, of course I am. She says that we're not here to attribute blame, but to find out what the real problem is.

CATHY: So what I'm hearing is this: you, Arthur, see Barbara as the main problem, especially in her recent change of moods; and you, Barbara, find Arthur intolerant and unapproachable. Have I heard you correctly?

ARTHUR: Yes, that sounds fair.

BARBARA: That's about it.

CATHY: It all sounds a bit like a circle, or the 'chicken and the egg' syndrome. I'm wondering what came first: Arthur's intolerance or Barbara's change of moods? It might help if you could tell me when these changes in your relationship first became noticeable by you both.

ARTHUR: It's been going on for about a year now – you'd come home from school exhausted, often with a headache and drained of all energy. You'd be flopped on the sofa when I got home from work, and ask me to get the meal. That happened on a number of occasions, didn't it?

BARBARA: Yes. I thought it was my job that was getting me down.

CATHY: Had there been any changes at work, Barbara, to account for your sudden exhaustion?

BARBARA: None that I can think of. It was about the time that Ivy (she's one of the staff) went on maternity leave. Apart from that, nothing important I can think of.

CATHY: Ivy went on maternity leave. Are you very friendly with her?

BARBARA: She was always full of fun, and very good company. Yes, I suppose I did miss her when she left.

CATHY: How did you feel about her having a baby?

BARBARA: I wondered how she'd cope with her job *and* a new baby. . . .

CATHY: Yes, but how did *you* feel about her having a baby?

BARBARA: Feel? Just normal.

CATHY: Well, what feelings are normal for you concerning Ivy's new baby?

BARBARA: I suppose you want me to say I was envious, don't you?

CATHY: No, Barbara, I don't want you to say anything other than what your true feelings were at that time.

BARBARA: It's just that the family are always asking me, 'When are you going to start a family?' I'm sick of it.

CATHY: Whose family?

ARTHUR: It's mine, really. Barbara's lost her parents.

CATHY: So you're saying that you're sick of Arthur's family asking when you're going to start a family. Is that right, Barbara.

BARBARA: They go on and on about it, that's all.

CATHY: What would you like to say to them about that?

BARBARA: I'd like to say, 'Mind your own bloody business!'

CATHY: You sound angry with them.

BARBARA: I suppose I am.

CATHY: Do you find it hard to express your anger, Barbara?

BARBARA: Well, it's not very nice, is it? I mean, you can't go around getting angry all the time, can you?

CATHY: You appear to be uneasy about your angry feelings. I wonder what you do with all that anger you feel towards your in-laws?

ARTHUR: She avoids them, mostly – my parents, I mean.

BARBARA: I suppose I do.

CATHY: So you try to avoid your anger by avoiding your in-laws?

BARBARA: It seems best.

CATHY: For whom? Best for whom?

BARBARA: Best all round.

CATHY: What you're saying, then, is something like this: you'd like to say to your in-laws, 'Mind your own bloody business!' but you avoid saying this by keeping out of their way.

BARBARA: You're right. I hate rows.

CATHY: Let's go back a bit. You avoided telling me how you felt about Ivy having a baby. You seemed to expect that you should feel envious about that. So I wonder if you usually avoid your feelings altogether?

BARBARA: I'm not an emotional person, I suppose.

ARTHUR: She doesn't often lose her temper.

CATHY: I wonder if there's a connection, then, between your not feeling right, as Arthur said, and your not expressing your feelings? You see, Barbara, I don't think it's true that you're not an emotional person: if you're human you possess the full range of human emotions just like anyone else.

BARBARA: Oh, Arthur: I wish we'd never come here! Do we have to stay?

ARTHUR: We've come for help, haven't we? It's not going to help if you just walk away from what Cathy is saying, is it?

CATHY: Barbara, you say you wish you'd never come here tonight. Can you say what is happening to you right now?

BARBARA: I feel on edge. I'm not used to talking like this.

CATHY: I understand that. It's not easy to come here and take a risk by talking about yourself at this level. Your edgy feelings seem to be in response to my suggestion that there might be a connection between your not feeling right and your not expressing your feelings. Is that so?

BARBARA: You may be right.

CATHY: It's not important that I'm right, Barbara; it's far more important for you to become aware of your inner feelings and start to express them.

ARTHUR: Can I butt in here? Look, Babs, you often tell me everything's OK when it's perfectly obvious that everything's *not* OK. You don't often talk about the way you feel; you just shrug it off as if it's not important. And there are times when I just feel shut out by you.

CATHY: What do you do with your shut-out feelings, Arthur?

ARTHUR: I just read my paper, or go out into the garden. I think it's best to leave her alone.

CATHY: What effect does that have on you, Barbara?

BARBARA: I feel abandoned and rejected. That's what I meant when I said he was unapproachable.

CATHY: It sounds a bit like this: Arthur asks you how you feel; you won't tell him how you feel, and just 'shrug off' his enquiry; then, Arthur reads his paper or goes out into the garden, and you end up feeling rejected, and then blame Arthur for rejecting you.

ARTHUR: That's it! I usually end up feeling the fault's all mine. I'm beginning to see that that isn't so.

BARBARA: So what you're *both* saying to me is that it's all my fault?

CATHY: Barbara, neither I nor Arthur have suggested that. We are not here to establish blame on anyone – just to find out what is happening between you that is making you both so unhappy.

ARTHUR: So where do we go from here?

CATHY: It seems to me that neither of you is really being honest with the other about your feelings. There sounds to be a lot of things going on inside both of you which you are not telling your partner.

BARBARA: There's no point in upsetting people with your feelings, is there?

CATHY You believe that if you were honest with Arthur about your feelings, he would be upset?

BARBARA: Yes.

CATHY: Why don't you check that out with him; ask him which he would prefer: you hiding your feelings, or him being possibly upset?

BARBARA: Arthur, which would you prefer? For me to be open about the way I feel inside, and risk you being upset. Or, not telling you the way I feel and leaving things as they are?

ARTHUR: That's easy. I'd far rather you levelled with me about the way you're feeling, even at the risk of being upset.

CATHY: Arthur, you seem to be saying that you are prepared to take responsibility for the way you feel about the way Barbara feels; is that so?

ARTHUR: Certainly. At least everything would be out in the open where we can deal with it, rather than all this covering up. It's *that* I can't stand.

CATHY: Arthur is saying, if I understand you correctly, that you needn't conceal the way you feel inside; he's willing to take the risk. Are you, Barbara?

BARBARA: It's not easy – but I'll try.

CATHY: I understand it must be difficult for you to change the habits of a life-time, Barbara, but it might be worth the attempt. Arthur is saying he's willing to listen.

BARBARA: Where do I start?

CATHY: Let's go back to where we started. I asked you about your feelings about Ivy and her baby. Can you remember how you felt about that event?

BARBARA: Mixed-up feelings, really. Part of me was glad for her, of course, part of me was envious; and another part was scared.

CATHY: Scared? Scared of what?

BARBARA: Scared of what a baby might do to *me*, I think.

CATHY: Like what?

BARBARA: My mother told me I nearly killed her when I was born. 'You nearly did for me', she used to say. 'It's your fault I never had any more children!' That's what she told me when

I was young. I always thought, 'I'm not having children when I get married!' I know it sounds silly, but that's just what I thought.

CATHY: That doesn't sound silly to me at all, Barbara. It's what I would expect a frightened little girl to think about childbirth. Your mother was blaming you for something you weren't directly responsible for, wasn't she?

BARBARA: When you put it like that, I suppose so.

ARTHUR: This is news to me, Babs. You've never told me that before. I always thought it was because of your career and the mortgage that you didn't want kids.

CATHY: But that isn't true, is it, Barbara? You said just now you felt envious about Ivy having a baby. That means that somewhere inside you, you actually would like a baby?

BARBARA: Yes, Cathy. I realize I've not exactly been honest with you, Arthur, about children. It was just easier to tell you a white lie instead.

CATHY: But you still have to face your fear, don't you Barbara?

BARBARA: Yes. How can I do that?

CATHY: Well, it might be a good place to start with your mother's story. Do you honestly believe that you are to blame for her not having any more children?

BARBARA: She told me as much.

CATHY: But, do *you* believe that to be true?

BARBARA: Well, no, I don't. I can't see how I have to be blamed for what happened to my mother. After all, I didn't ask to be born, did I? She must take some responsibility for that, surely?

ARTHUR: That sounds right to me, Babs. Fancy telling you that story when you were little, and frightening you like that. Your mother ought to be ashamed of herself!

BARBARA: But, she's not here now, is she? It's not right to speak about her like that, seeing what happened to her and dad.

CATHY: Barbara, Arthur said a while ago that you'd lost your parents. Could you say a a bit more about how that happened?

BARBARA: It was last year – yes, about a year ago. They were going on their holidays, and they were in collision with an articulated lorry that went out of control. It wasn't their fault.

CATHY: How did you feel about what happened to them, Barbara?

BARBARA: I couldn't believe it at the time. After all, we'd only said goodbye to them a few hours before it happened. I never thought it would be . . . the last time I'd see them.

ARTHUR: Now then, Babs, don't upset yourself!

CATHY: Arthur, you said just now that you were willing to accept the risk of being upset by what Barbara had to say to you. Can you allow Barbara to 'get upset' about the death of her parents?

ARTHUR: You don't forget much, do you?

CATHY: It's part of my task to listen attentively to you both, Arthur. By telling Barbara not to upset herself, you are doing precisely the opposite of what you told her to do a moment ago, that was to speak freely about her feelings.

BARBARA: I *am* upset about my parents' death. At their funeral everyone was telling me to be brave, and not to let the family down by crying. I just buried it all – and the others said how good I was. They seemed to reward me for being false. I was crying inside but no one noticed. That's why I find it hard to blame my mother now for what she told me as a child.

CATHY: So, what you're saying Barbara is this: you've never really grieved about your parents' death?

BARBARA: I don't think I ever have. Is that why I've been feeling so sad without really knowing why?

CATHY: Certainly. If our deepest feelings get suppressed in the way yours were, we might have the *event* out of our minds, but we carry the *feelings* appropriate to that event around with us all the time. I often think of it as a kind of emotional shadow we live in. It seems to cast its effect over us without recognizing the reality behind it. Like your parents' death.

ARTHUR: That makes a lot of sense to me. But I still don't understand where not having a baby comes into it.

CATHY: Wasn't that another kind of shadow, Barbara – the shadow of feeling responsible for mother not having another baby, because of the way she placed that responsibility on to you?

BARBARA: It certainly felt like that. I guess I've always felt responsible for mother's unhappiness. But I've never really understood why – until now.

ARTHUR: Do you mean to say that events that long ago can still go on affecting us today? I mean, I can see where Babs' losing her parents can affect her – after all that was only a year ago – but the way she was born? That sounds a bit far-fetched to me!

BARBARA: But that's just how it felt, Arthur. It was ingrained in my childhood. It made me feel I owed mother something that was never quite defined. It was a feeling – that's all.

ARTHUR: If your mother put the blame for not having any more children on to you, like I said before, I think she ought to be ashamed of herself. That's cruel.

BARBARA: Arthur! How can I do that now that she's gone? It would seem like stamping on her grave!

CATHY: I hear that there's two things bothering you, Barbara. One is the death of your parents, your dad too, not just mum; the other is to find a way of considering having a family free from the fear of childbirth which your mother instilled into you. Does that sound right?

BARBARA: Yes.

CATHY: Perhaps it might help if you looked for a while at how you felt (and feel) about losing your dad.

BARBARA: Being the youngest, the baby of the family, I always felt I was his pride and joy. Don't get me wrong – he didn't dislike my sister Mary; he was fair to both of us. It's just that there was always a strong rapport between me and dad. We seemed to understand one another in a way mum and I never did.

CATHY: You sound very close to your father.

BARBARA: I am – was. I know it's hard to say this, and I feel guilty about saying it, but it's dad that I miss now, not mum. Oh, she was all right, but there was nothing close there for me. Whenever I went to see them, it was always dad I wanted to see. He'd take me out and show me his garden – he had a wonderful garden – and talk about what he'd been doing, and what he'd planted. He'd ask me about school, and how things were going; he just took an interest in me and what I was doing, in a way that mum never did. She somehow seemed to resent our relationship. She never noticed how she and Mary would have their private chats, ignoring me and dad. She seemed to treat Mary as her favourite, and I suppose dad did the same with me. He was so looking forward to his retirement and to what he was going to do with his spare time. I never thought when I said goodbye to them for their holidays I'd never see them again. It's so . . . unfair.

CATHY: How do you feel at this moment, Barbara. You appear to be sad as you talk about dad.

BARBARA: I feel it's all such a waste . . . he wasn't an old man . . . he had so much to live for . . . just . . . wiped out! (*Barbara starts to cry . . .*)

ARTHUR: Come on, love.

CATHY: Can you give Barbara permission to cry, instead of talking her out of what she wants to do?

ARTHUR: I hate to see her upset. It upsets me to watch her cry.

CATHY: Arthur, do you never cry?

ARTHUR: It's not manly to cry.

CATHY: Who taught you that?

ARTHUR: My dad. He taught me that big boys don't cry.

CATHY: So what do big boys do with their tears they don't cry?

ARTHUR: We just don't notice them.

CATHY: You pretend, in other words?

ARTHUR: Well, if you want to put it like that, yes.

CATHY: What way would you put it then, Arthur?

ARTHUR: We just teach ourselves not to cry. It's not done.

CATHY: So by teaching yourself not to cry, you put being brave above being honest. Is that it?

ARTHUR: In my family, yes. But I've never thought of it as being dishonest.

CATHY: How *have* you thought of it?

ARTHUR: Being manly.

CATHY: So, if I've heard you correctly, you're saying that you never allow yourself to cry since it's not manly to cry. How, then, does that fit in with your not wanting your wife to cry? Do you expect her to be as manly as you?

ARTHUR: I've not looked at it that way. I just get upset to see her upset, that's all.

CATHY: But, Arthur, that is not all, is it? You don't see any connection between your refusal to show your own emotions, and your refusal to allow Barbara to show hers?

ARTHUR: I don't refuse her. . . .

CATHY: But you make it perfectly clear, as you did a moment ago, that you do not like her to cry in front of you.

BARBARA: Can I butt in here . . .

CATHY: Sure.

BARBARA: Arthur, you have never seemed to be able to cope with my emotions. You appear so cold at times, and don't really appreciate the way I feel. If I start to talk to you about the way I feel, you change the subject, or walk away, or tell me not to get so 'emotional'. What Cathy has just said, I've been feeling for years now, only I've never found the words to express myself. Cathy has put into words exactly how you come across to me at times, and she's only just met you.

CATHY: So, when you said at the beginning that you weren't an emotional person, that wasn't really true, was it? Perhaps what you meant was that you had got out of the habit of expressing to Arthur the way you feel sometimes?

BARBARA: Oh dear, I never thought all this would come out!

CATHY: I noticed when I mentioned this to you before, that you appeared very uneasy. You said you wished you'd never come here tonight, didn't you? Being honest with one another appears to be very hard for both of you.

BARBARA: I didn't realize so much was wrong between us, that's all. I thought it was just me . . .

CATHY: That's what Arthur said right at the beginning, didn't you Arthur? You said, the trouble was with Barbara, that she 'wasn't right'.

ARTHUR: So you're trying to pin all the blame on to me, are you?

CATHY: Arthur, counselling is not about pinning the blame on to anyone. As a matter of fact I believe that it's not necessarily either your or Barbara who is in the wrong. It's the way you are *relating* to one another that needs attention. The problem appears to me to be in the old style of relating that you have been used to. It has been based on a kind of agreement between you two, that any display of emotions is not to be allowed. So you get upset if Barbara gets upset, and because Barbara wants to please you, she conceals her true feelings, bottling them up until finally they couldn't find any more room in the bottle, and she burst!

BARBARA: So I'm not to blame for what has happened?

CATHY: Not as far as I can see, Barbara. What fault there is appears to be in the style of relating which is no longer working for either of you.

ARTHUR: Can you say a bit more about our 'style of relating'? I'm not sure I've got your drift.

CATHY: What I mean is this. When two people marry, they begin a new phase of their relationship. This requires many adjustments on both sides, getting to know one another well, and what makes each other tick. Because of a natural desire to please, we usually try and fit in with what the other person wants. In your case, you have made it clear, Arthur, that the direct expression of emotions bothers you, so Barbara has learnt to suppress these feelings. Funnily enough, this is just what her family was doing to her at the funeral of her parents. She was told to be brave, and not let the family down by crying. That must have sounded like an echo of what you have been telling Barbara for years. And you told her that because that was how you were brought up. Since you couldn't really cope with your own feelings by any other means than denial, you expected Barbara to do the same. If you like, there was an unwritten agreement or 'script' to your marriage, which reads: 'No feelings, please; we're Browns!'

BARBARA: Well, you've certainly put that clearly for me, Cathy. So what you're implying is that we've *both* got to change, not just me?

ARTHUR: This style of relating, then, or 'script' as you call it, needs changing. How ought we to do this?

CATHY: First, let me respond to your 'got to', Barbara, and that 'ought' of yours, Arthur, so that we are clear about how we proceed. There is no 'got to' coming from me, Barbara, since I'm not here to tell either of you what to do or what not to do. I can only help to reflect the consequences of your present style of relating to each other, and how that seems to be affecting you both. Any changes are for you two to decide upon, not me. The choice is entirely yours. I can help, of course, in helping you to find a new 'script' for your marriage, but it's really up to you what you do with that. Then there's your 'ought', Arthur. 'Ought' implies 'I owe it', and you are not indebted to any counsellor since they have no magic wands. There is only your decision; that's what makes it right. It's important for the two of you to find what is right *for you*.

BARBARA: I'm happy with that. It makes it a lot clearer to me.

ARTHUR: Me too.

CATHY: As we're coming to the end of our session, perhaps it might help if I attempt to sum up how far we've got tonight?

ARTHUR: Are we in for a long period of counselling?

CATHY: I don't really know, Arthur. I believe that we have made some progress tonight, and I'm happy to work with you until you feel you have enough to work on by yourselves.

BARBARA: I see.

CATHY: Well, there seems to be a real issue in the legacy your mother left you, Barbara, concerning responsibility for her not having any more children. Connected to that is the question of your fear of childbirth, and you will need to look at that rather closely. For instance, you might need to discover ways in which you can disconnect those fears from those of a frightened child and look at this question from the standpoint of your adult awareness and learning. Next, there's the question of your parents' death. You do seem to have some 'unfinished business' in connection with that tragic event. Then, for both of you, there's the question of how to express your feelings – both of you – to one another. Arthur needs to tackle his childhood script of being a 'big brave boy' in order to please father. That has left you, Arthur, with an impairment in your self-expression. You will not really be able to relate to the way Barbara feels until you relate more adequately to the way you feel inside yourself.

BARBARA: It all seems so clear when you put it that way.

ARTHUR: So the changes are going to be the ones we decide upon.

CATHY: Yes, Arthur.

BARBARA: Is there anything for us to be doing meanwhile?

CATHY: Well, there's the need for you to start telling one another how you feel. Try not to protect one another from your own feelings. *Allow* the other person to be upset by what you say about the way you feel. It's so easy to take responsibility for the way the other person feels but this is not really necessary or helpful.

ARTHUR: You mean, we're to be more honest and open with each other?

CATHY: It seems a good place to start, Arthur. You will then be taking the first steps in changing the way you relate to one another.

BARBARA: The first of many, perhaps?

CATHY: Perhaps.

ARTHUR: Anything is worth trying – it has to be better than it is now.

CATHY: Before you both go, could you each say how this first session has been for you?

ARTHUR: Well, it's been an eye-opener, that's for sure. I came in here an hour ago thinking something was wrong with Babs. Now I'm going out seeing that I'm part of the trouble – that I need to change as well as Babs. It's also helped by unloading all this stuff – I must say, I couldn't make head or tail of it all, but you Cathy seemed to know what was happening. Maybe I'm too close to it all?

BARBARA: I had no idea that there was any connection between the way I've been feeling and those events long ago. It's been like opening a family scrap-book and seeing all those childhood images coming back to me. I know I have been denying my feelings, chiefly for Art's sake, but also for my own. I've not wanted to see him upset.

CATHY: Thank you both for being so honest tonight. I realize this has not been an easy session for either of you. You've been ready to face some unpleasant truths about yourselves, and that's always a risk. I'm glad you were ready to take those risks, in order to improve the quality of your relationship. You seem to have so much going for both of you, and by identifying the real underlying issues here tonight, we have made a start towards a new way of relating and, hopefully, in the quality of your own happiness too. I'll see you the same time next week. Goodbye, Barbara; goodbye, Arthur.

BOTH: Goodnight – and thanks.

This verbatim account of Cathy's first session with the Browns is not intended as a definitive model of how such sessions *ought* to go; rather, it shows how it *might* have gone. Frankly, Cathy and the Browns got much further in this session than most first sessions would have accomplished. Counselling has to go at the speed the clients can manage; this dialogue showed how the various issues were identified and in part examined by the counsellor, and already we can see various parts of the agenda which further sessions would explore in greater depth.

Cathy was applying most of the principles taught her in her counselling training: not to give advice, or to do for them what they could well do for themselves. The natural anxieties of both counsellor and the couple were obvious at the beginning of the session, but they all seem to have relaxed a bit more once the dialogue got under way. Cathy was in no way telling the Browns how to run their marriage; she emphasized their power of choice, and confronted them with their avoidance techniques. She was faithful to her role as an enabler, and what came out in this session laid the ground for future sessions. Some counsellors might work a little slower, and would want to get to know the couple a bit better, to 'get a feel' of what their relationship style was, before getting into the problems under the surface. These emerged quite clearly: Arthur's inability to cope with feelings, his own as well as Barbara's; Barbara's protection of Arthur in consequence of this, together with her quandary as to what to do with her deeply suppressed feelings of grief for her parents, and the dilemma that Ivy's baby presented to her. Cathy showed how 'non-possessive warmth' can work out in practice, and her own style of 'creative distancing' was about right.

The important issue of blame was carefully explained in this dialogue by Cathy, and she was right to emphasize that it was *their style of relating* which needed attention. Since both would be responsible for this style, they could both relax a little and try harder to listen to their partners, free from guilt. Also, the important matter of their own on-going work at their marriage was pointed out by the counsellor. No miracles are going to happen, at least not in the counselling hour itself, and each needs to take back into the week, before their next appointment, something to work at by way of seeking improvement in their situation. Some couples bring their problems and want to dump them in the counsellor's lap and say, 'There's a mess – we'll let you clear it up. You're the expert!' It simply doesn't work out that way, for the reasons explained earlier. Counselling is not an easy option whereby couples can opt out of their responsibility for their own marriage; the counsellor is there to help you see more clearly what the problems really consist of, and what work *you* need to do in order to improve your marriage.

19
The counselling contract

By 'contract', I am not referring to a legally binding and enforceable agreement between the counsellor and the client/s. But while counselling does not work on the basis of a legal contract, common sense demands that there be some basis of agreement between the parties as to what the whole counselling enterprise is about.

While individual counsellors and counselling agencies may have their own variations, here are some of the main points that counsellors and clients need to include in their basis of agreement to work together:

1. Confidentiality

Counselling involves the disclosure of one's deepest thoughts, feelings and personal history. This is best done with the knowledge that such information remains confidential to the counsellor. Most counsellors will volunteer that fact at the beginning of the counselling relationship, but if you are in any doubt, check this out with your counsellor. All of the larger counselling agencies (e.g. British Association for Counselling, Westminster Pastoral Foundation, Catholic Marriage Advisory Council, RELATE) have systems of accreditation for their counsellors which includes strong emphasis on confidentiality. Where clinical material is used for purposes of publication (as in this book) it is understood that the identity of the client is adequately disguised.

2. *Ethics*

The behaviour of counsellors towards their clients is also governed by Codes of Ethics set up by all the major counselling and accrediting agencies. These specifically deal with the respect and dignity afforded to those who come for counselling.

3. *Boundaries*

The counselling relationship usually operates along the lines of other professional services such as doctors. Since the contract is with the person (or couple) who come for counselling, contact with (and by) other members of the family are usually not encouraged. The keeping of boundaries concerns chiefly the matter of time. Punctuality is usually expected; cancellations of appointments are expected rather than non-appearance at a pre-arranged time; and the length of each appointment is usually agreed at the outset. The counsellor will be responsible for the management of these boundaries. Contacts with counsellors outside these agreed appointments is usually not encouraged.

4. *Payment of fees*

The amount and the frequency of payments will be discussed with you at the outset. As in other areas of counselling, honesty about your circumstances will be welcomed. Most counsellors operate on a pay-as-you-go policy.

5. *Expectations*

The counsellor will share with you what his or her expectations are concerning what your sessions will be about, and you will be invited to share your expectations of the counsellor. One writer helpfully explains how he puts this to his clients:

> In these sessions you will be exploring your own experience. I am just here to help you to do that, by offering the time and space you need. I can offer certain skills which may enable you to do it better or quicker than you could on your own, but basically it is you doing it, not me doing it. And unless you really treat it in that way, nothing much is going to change.[37]

6. Duration

It is impossible to say at the commencement of the counselling process how long 'it' will take, since no one knows at this point what 'it' is! Some counsellors agree with their clients to attend a certain number of sessions (say six) which gives the process time to work. After that, a new contract can be agreed based on the needs which are beginning to surface in the couple concerned. Should the counsellor feel that either the couple is getting nowhere, or that they may be better off with another counsellor, they will say this.

7. Referral

In the case of the counsellor becoming aware that another counsellor would be more qualified or is specifically trained in an area the couple is exploring (say, psycho-sexual counselling) they will offer to make a referral on their behalf. This is not unusual; counsellors are responsible for the best way of supplying help to people, just as doctors make referrals to other doctors (consultants) in the best interests of their patients. This need not be interpreted as incompetence in the counsellor, or rejection of the clients.

8. Responsibility

Couples in counselling are responsible for themselves. The counsellor is responsible for being 'fully present' for the couple just as s/he will invite the couple to be fully present at the sessions. The counsellor is not a rescuer, nor does the outcome of the counselling process depend on him/her. Changes always reside within the couple's own competence, and will be solely determined by them.

9. Changing counsellor

No one can expect to help everyone. There are certain occasions when the counsellor and the couple simply don't 'mix'. The reasons for this are usually unconscious but it is a truth of life. Issues of incompatability are not the exclusive possession of the husbands and wives! The three people involved can choose to work on discovering what issues lie beneath the antipathy towards one another, but often it happens that a change of counsellor is the accepted way out. If it occurs that you are always finding that counsellors are 'just like my mother/father', this may indicate that you need to stay long enough to find out what you are projecting on to your helpers.

10. Terminating the contract

Most of us are reluctant to face endings of any kind, because they involve a kind of 'death'. In the case of fixed-term contracts, the couple will know when the ending is to be. In cases of longer periods of counselling, over several years say, there is a need to plan for the ending of the counselling relationship, and to deal with the issues which this ending will provoke in the couple themselves. Like midwives, counsellors are but transitional figures and they have to cope with letting go of those in whom they have seen new life and growth.[38]

You do not have to approach counselling blind. You have the right to express to your counsellor your doubts and fears, and to make your feelings and uncertainties known to them. The 'therapeutic alliance', as it is sometimes called, is a unique kind of relationship between you and your partner and your counsellor. While friendly, it is not friendship. It is about seeking particular help at a particular time in your life. Counsellors, as 'emotional AA men/women', are there to assist you in getting back on your journey through life.

Conclusion

This journey into the world of counselling may have been a strange one for some of you. I have tried to lead you through the hitherto alien paths which 'going into counselling' entails. For most people, such paths might remain untrodden territory, since they have found creative ways of leading their lives and of dealing with their most important relationships. Such fortunate people may regard counselling as for 'them', not 'us'. However, it is sometimes found to be a very short distance between them and us, when an unmanageable crisis bursts in upon our otherwise tranquil world. For those of us whose life appears strewn with thorns and boulders, too much for us to handle alone, counselling becomes not just an option but a necessity. When we have exhausted our own ideas and resources, and made Herculean attempts to find our own solutions, what other avenues are there for us to turn to? I trust that this consumer's guide has at least pointed you in the direction of help, and the barriers you must overcome before seeking it.

You have followed me so far in attempting to answer four of the most important questions regarding counselling: How does counselling work? Who needs counselling? What problems do people bring to counselling? and, What happens at a counselling session? As we have examined these questions we have encountered ordinary people suffering from normal human misery. No one, and no social grouping, has a monopoly on misery. In spite of responding to the daily temptation of advertising and television commercials offering an illusory world of false happiness, based on the 'More – and bigger – is better' falsehood, we find in the end that we are still as unhappy as we were before we went down that dead-end path. The pursuit of wealth has replaced our pursuit of happiness; fools as we are, we have mistaken the one for the other. Possessions have become the desired objects for most of us, and instead of using things and loving people, we find ourselves *using people* and *loving things*.

Many of the people I counsel day by day are at the very peak of their careers. They have reached the heights that lesser mortals merely dream about. They are often the object of envy in society in terms of status, income and life-style. Yet they confess to me their own inner sadness, and disillusionment. They have tried all the substitutes for happiness this world can offer, and they have come away empty. They have never come to terms with their deepest inner reality, that self which is crying out for recognition and acceptance. The truth appears to be that, in order for us to become fully human and fully alive, we need to find our deepest longings and aspirations not in the heights (of fame, position or income) but in the depths of our own being. Lacking a grounding in self-love and acceptance, we are unable to build anything substantial by way of self-fulfilment. Here lies much of the raw material for later disillusionment and unhappiness. Our basic need is to find a self to be true to.

The mistake we then make is to attach this need to a relationship with a significant other. Lacking a sense of selfhood, we must seek self-fulfilment through another person, and it is now *their* responsibility to make us happy. When they fail in this task – as inevitably they must, despite their efforts to meet our expectations or demands – they then bear the blame for our own unhappiness. It is very often at this point that counselling becomes a real need in order to sort out what is going wrong in the relationship. In our current social climate this is becoming a normal, if not necessary, thing to do.

I have welcomed the abandonment of the former suspicion that has sometimes been associated with counselling and the counselled. Such attitudes sprang out of ignorance rather than experience. In increasing numbers people are breaking through the specifically British phobia of being thought of as mentally ill or totally inadequate, and seeking the help of trained people who will listen sympathetically to their problem. RELATE alone provided 264,000 counselling sessions in 1987. I hope I have said enough in this book to encourage others to seek help when they need it, and what the implications might be for them should they do so.

However, there is another attitude towards counselling which also needs to be mentioned. This concerns the myth that counselling is an infallible magic wand; one wave, and our world is put right again! We must beware of setting counselling up as a behavioural cure-all, and counsellors as wizards or magicians. Counselling is not about 'doing things to people'; it is about helping people to do things for themselves. It is about affirming people's rights to determine their own existence and choices – even their own misery – without being treated as weak or worthless. Counselling is always about the possibility of change in our circumstances by making different choices in our lives, and different responses in our most important relationships. Far from creating a new form of elitist dependence, counselling aims at the creation of independence and interdependence, and finding how we can grasp the nettle of taking responsibility for ourselves within that process of change. Counsellors do not aim at producing people like themselves. Although they will model for others an alternative pattern of behaving and responding, and how an honest yet caring relationship might look like, their aim is always to help people to *be* themselves. As Carl Jung once said to a friend, 'I do not want anybody to be a Jungian; I want people above all to be themselves.'[39].

So entering into a counselling relationship is like starting out on a journey. It is essentially a journey in company with a trained guide who knows a bit about the terrain to be covered, its pitfalls, swamps and quagmires – it's likely that the counsellor has been in many of them himself. At the very least, the counsellor/guide knows most of the blind alleys and behavioural cul-de-sacs down which people travel seeking a remedy to their problems. As with other journeys, no one can do this task for us; no one can take a journey for anyone else by proxy. We might make the journey *with* someone, but never *for* someone. That would be like eating a meal for someone else. At any point, the traveller may turn back, finding the going too rough, the implications too threatening, the changes too demanding, or the possible outcome alarming. At such points, the guide informs the traveller that he has a choice, and assures him that no one is going to force anyone to go where they do not choose to go. Freud used to speak to his patients about their terminating the treatment unilaterally, warning that to do so would ensure their going back to the prison from whence they have come. The counsellor/guide will remind the traveller of why they set out in the first place, what they sought relief from, and will ask them to consider whether that is really what they want to go back to. In the final analysis, however, it is the traveller's choice – and the traveller's responsibility.

Like many of the familiar mythical journeys – that of Odysseus, for example – there are many perils to face on the journey home. Indeed, the story of Odysseus is, in many ways, the story of every man's and every woman's journey of personal transformation. The couples who start out on the journey of counselling will discover, as Odysseus did, the monsters which lie on their path and the temptations (as the Siren voices tempted Odysseus) to abandon the whole enterprise of returning home. Many couples, however, stop their ears to such allurements, and risk the difficulties which counselling sometimes entails. Arriving 'home', however, most of us would say that the journey had been worth while.

Although writing about the journey of Odysseus back to Ithaca, the Greek poet C. P. Cavafy might have been thinking of the journey through counselling when he wrote:

> Ithaca has given you the beautiful voyage.
> Without her you would never have taken the road.
> But she had nothing more to give you.
> And if you find her poor, Ithaca has not defrauded you.
> With the great wisdom you have gained,
> With so much experience
> You must surely have understood by then
> What Ithacas mean.[40]

Bon voyage!

Notes

1. Sheldon Kopp, *If You meet the Buddha on the Road, Kill Him!* (Sheldon Press 1979), p. 16f.
2. John Donne, *Devotions* XVII.
3. Kopp, *op. cit.*, p.78.
4. Quoted in L. LeShan, *Holistic Health* (Turnstone Press 1984), p. 61.
5. M. Scott Peck, *The Road Less Travelled* (Simon & Schuster 1978), p. 174f.
6. Quoted in *Changes*, vol. 4, no. 4, October 1986.
7. Karl Menninger, *Theory of Psychoanalytic Technique* (Harper & Row 1958), p. 85.
8. Kopp, *op. cit.*, p. 17.
9. *Ibid.*, p. 2.
10. John Rowan, *The Reality Game* (Routledge 1983), p. 38.
11. Kopp, *op. cit.*, p. 140.
12. Christopher F. Clulow, *Marital Therapy* (Aberdeen University Press 1985), p. 3.
13. Scott Peck, *op.cit.*, pp. 84–5.
14. S. Naifeh and G. White Smith, *Why Can't Men Open Up?* (Sphere Books 1985), p. 5.
15. L. S. Groh and B. Lane, 'Overcoming the Peter Pan Syndrome', *The Journal of Pastoral Care*, vol. XLII, no. 1 (Spring 1988), p. 39.
16. Naifeh and White Smith, *op. cit.*, p. 7.
17. William Bridges, *Transitions* (Addison Wesley 1980), p. 90.
18. Erich Fromm, *The Art of Loving* (Unwin Books 1975), pp. 53–4.
19. Scott Peck, *op. cit.*, p. 81.
20. Fromm, *op. cit.*, p. 54.
21. Alexander Lowen, *Narcissism: Denial of the True Self* (Collier Books 1985), p. 31.
22. Quoted in *The Times*, 1 February 1988.
23. From *The Paul Simon Song Book*, Pattern Music, 1965.

24. Paul Tournier, *Marriage Difficulties* (SCM Press 1971), p. 14.
25. Kahlil Gibran, *The Prophet* (Heinemann 1976), p. 19.
26. Madonna Kolbenschlag, *Kiss Sleeping Beauty Goodbye* (Harper & Row 1979), p. xi.
27. Sam Keen, *The Passionate Life* (Gateway Books 1985), p. 9.
28. James Nelson, *Embodiment* (SPCK 1978), p. 146.
29. *Ibid.*, p. 147.
30. Jack Dominian, *Proposals for a New Sexual Ethic* (Darton, Longman & Todd 1977), p. 65.
31. Nelson, *op. cit.*, p. 148.
32. Quoted in William Barclay, *Ethics in a Permissive Society* (Fontana Books 1971), p. 77.
33. Daniel Levinson, *Seasons of a Man's Life* (Ballantine Books 1978), p. 60f.
34. *Ibid.*, p. 200.
35. Gail Sheehy, *Passages* (Corgi 1977).
36. Gail Sheehy, *Pathfinders* (Sidgwick & Jackson 1982).
37. John Rowan, *op. cit.*, p. 35.
38. See also my paper, 'Termination of the Counsellor-Client Relationship: Factors in Ending the Contract', in *Counselling*, the Journal of the British Association for Counselling, no. 48, May 1984.
39. Laurens van der Post, *Jung and the Story of our Time* (Penguin 1986), p. x.
40. From 'Ithaca', *The Complete Poems of Cavafy*, trans. Rae Dalven (Hogarth Press 1961).

Further reading

Marriage, Faith and Love, Jack Dominian (Darton Longman & Todd, 1981)
Marital Therapy: an inside view, Christopher Clulow (Aberdeen University Press, 1985)
Women Men Love, Women Men Leave, Connell Cowan and Melvyn Kinder (Signet, 1987)
The Peter Pan Syndrome, Dan Kiley (Avon, 1983)
What do Women Want?, Luise Eichenbaum and Susie Orbach (Fontana, 1983)
Marital Therapy in Britain, ed. Windy Dryden (2 vols, Harper & Row, 1985)
The Road Less Travelled, M. Scott Peck (Century Paperback, new edn 1988)
Make or Break?, Jack Dominian (SPCK, 1984)
Couples Arguing, Tony Gough (Darton, Longman & Todd, 1987)

Marriage counselling agencies

Among the professional agencies who specialize in couples counselling are:

RELATE (The National Marriage Guidance Council),
Head Office:
Herbert Gray College,
Little Church Street,
Rugby,
Warwickshire CV21 3AP (tel. 0788 73241)
or see in your local telephone directory under RELATE.

The Catholic Marriage Advisory Council,
15 Lansdowne Road,
Holland Park,
London W11 3AJ (tel. 01–727 0141)

The British Association for Counselling,
37A Sheep Street,
Rugby,
Warwickshire CV21 3BX (tel. 0788 78328–9)
(The BAC produce an up-to-date directory of counsellors in various parts of the country, most of whom offer marital counselling.)

COMPASS (Counselling on Merseyside – Pastoral and Supporting Service),
25 Hope Street,
Liverpool,
Merseyside L1 9BQ (tel. 051–708 6688)
(As a general rule, COMPASS counsellors only see individuals, rather than couples.)

Scargill House,
Kettlewell,
Skipton,
N. Yorkshire BD23 5HU (tel. 075 676 234)
(This conference centre offers many programmes of Christian counselling and marriage enrichment. Send for the current brochure for full details.)

The Westminster Pastoral Foundation,
23 Kensington Square,
London W8 5HN (tel. 01–937 6956).
(The WPF have counselling centres around the country most of which offer marital counselling.)

Index